DUALITY

MY JOURNEY THROUGH DARKNESS INTO THE LIGHT

Liz-Ulrica

© Liz-Ulrica 2022

Duality

Published by Duality Publishing

Cape Town, South Africa

Tel: 063 582 5692

ISBN 978-0-620-99587-0

eSIBN 978-0-620-99588-7

4 6 8 10 9 7 5 3

Layout and cover design by Boutique Books

WHAT A JOURNEY! IT SEEMS like yesterday that I sat on this very same stone bench, on the banks of the most beautiful spot in the world, Lake Como. Time had stood still; nothing had changed since I had first laid eyes on it.

I gaze out over the shimmering, turquoise waters, watching the local ferry scuttling between villages, picking up and dropping off tourists. A family of ducks, paddle towards the reeds creating ripples on an otherwise calm surface. The gentle sound of water lapping the verges is meditative yet simultaneously engages all my senses. In the distance, the Swiss Alps, picture box with their snow-tipped peaks against a brilliant blue sky herald a harsh winter. Regardless of season, I mused, I am now a part owner of it. Who would have thought?

It's a scene I've carried with me for twenty- six years. Since then, this paradise, with its immense beauty and tranquillity has never been far from my heart. My unconscious drive to reach this destination has been long and arduous but it does not detract from the feeling of utter amazement to realise that I had finally arrived.

It all began with Proposte, an exclusive annual textile exhibition held in the historic Villa Erba on Lake Como. I had wangled my way into the Export, feeling like a complete outsider, then meandered into the manicured gardens with a view of the lake. Sitting down on a stone bench, I had promised myself that one day, I would return to spend the latter part of my life in this paradise, little did I know what awaited me...

HISTORY

THE CONSTANTIA VALLEY HAS BEEN my home since 1994, when I returned home to the place where my ancestors lived and died. Once a peaceful and evergreen suburb, Constantia Valley is now the choice of wealthy, mostly white families with its former residents forced out, leaving behind the graves of their ancestors.

Every day for the past ten years, I've driven by the small graveyard tucked away at the end of Parish Road in Constantia. The private cemetery was a place of pride and pain. This small piece of land held so many unresolved memories and mysteries that I was never quite ready to face.

Whenever I passed the cemetery with its tall pine trees, something odd would stir inside me. An emotion of dread would grip my chest, knowing that my grandmother's last remains were buried there. On this gorgeous sunny day, I gave in to the urge to stop and brought my white Mercedes to a halt on the gravel path. A sudden urge to explore this quiet and desolate cemetery, which held the key to my buried childhood memories, seized me.

I was born during the early stages of apartheid, when chaos and suffering were still prevalent - evidenced by the stories my parents and neighbours told when they were forcibly removed from their homes by the government. Back then, my mother still had strong links with Constantia, having spent most of her childhood in the valley at the properties of her wealthy and educated uncles.

Constantia is now the valley of the rich and famous. Still, it was once home to many "coloured" families, mainly of Christian and Muslim faiths, which is why there are many Muslim cemeteries and shrines in the area. Coloureds, a name given to people of mixed race by the colonialist, all-white apartheid government of 1948, were predominantly from the Western Cape in Southern Africa. Together, the Christian and Muslim communities formed one ethnic group, Coloured. In 1950, the apartheid government enacted the Group Areas Act, which restricted ownership and residence among different population groups, thus dividing urban areas based on race and colour.

The cemetery is desolate, and the gravestones are in desperate need of cleaning and restoration. It seems the dead were buried and then forgotten as I have never witnessed anyone visiting or tending to a grave when I have passed. It made me realise how temporary life is; that when we die, perhaps we may live on in our loved one's memories, but that also fades with time. Carefully, I stepped out of my car to prevent myself from slipping on the loose stones in my black high heels.

As my mother proudly explained, this graveyard is a private cemetery that belongs to her family. Since hearing that, I'd wanted to be amongst the few privileged inhabitants to make this sacred part of the world my final resting place. Slowly I made my way around some of the tombstones and mounds bearing familiar family names. I searched for the ancestral names that defined the turmoil from which my present life had emerged. Finally, I spotted the word "Southgate", proudly displayed at the top of a few tombstones. I found my mother's two uncles, older brothers of Annie, my grandmother, whom I had briefly met before they had passed on.

Then I stumbled upon another grave that read, "In loving memory of my beloved wife Annie Southgate born 1846 died 1901". I assumed it was the grave of my great-grandmother.

I searched for her grave, this woman who rejected and denigrated me by making me believe that I was ugly because of my skin colour and thick curly hair. I struggled to find her grave but then remembered attending her funeral at this small cemetery. Finally, it dawned on me that her tombstone would bear her married surname. My search took on an urgency, as if my life depended on it. I fervently ran around, tripping over hidden gravestones and scratching my legs on twigs and dry branches; my breathing quickened, and my chest pulled tight. Something inside me spurred me on. I felt as though some higher force had taken hold of me.

Having spent a reasonable amount of time scouring the small cemetery I finally decided to give up the search. I slumped defeatedly onto a marble gravestone. Closing my eyes, I surrendered to the deeply buried memories of my childhood, as tears poured down my cheeks. I fully immersed myself in the emotions that engulfed me as I relived memories of the rejection, discrimination and shame I had suffered. Shuddering at the hostility and contempt my grandmother openly showed towards me when I had the misfortune to be in her presence. While my white siblings and mother visited her house, I was never allowed to enter and always stood outside her closed gate. I almost felt relieved when she died of old age at eighty-five.

In a state of blind rage, I wanted nothing more than to hit back at her. The rush of anger quickly morphed into deep-seated sorrow as raw grief overtook me. Heart-wrenching sobs erupted like a river bursting its banks. The pain I'd buried for so long came rushing back, as if it were yesterday, all directed at this woman who was only one of those instrumental in shaping my life. I sat sobbing for what seemed like an eternity. Passers-by probably assumed I was crying at the grave of a loved one. As tears continued to roll down my cheeks, I slowly walked back to my car and put on my Prada sunglasses to hide my swollen, puffy face.

Annie, my grandmother, was the youngest of three children and the only girl of a wealthy family, so she was spoiled and privileged. Annie and her brothers inherited their wealth from their parents.

This well-known family originated from the Dutch and British colony of St Helena Island. After the Spanish and Dutch occupied the island, the British took it over. The consequent interbreeding produced an extraordinary beauty within the Islanders, such as Annie, tall with golden bronze skin tones, a face with high cheekbones, and big brown eyes. As a result, St Helenians often made their way to the Cape, searching for better living conditions and opportunities.

I was not interested in my grandmother's history because, as a child, I hated her and would have nothing to do with her.

Annie and her two brothers, Alfred and Terence, were well educated. One became a priest and the other a school principal. They lived in the Constantia valley until they were brutally evicted and forced to settle lower down the valley, in the Retreat area. Annie married a white fisherman and produced eight offspring, with two of their sons following in their father's footsteps.

While Annie was determined that her daughters would marry white men, the eldest daughter absconded with a dark-skinned man. The second eldest committed the ultimate sin by marrying a Muslim man.

My grandmother, a formidable woman, ruled her family with an iron fist, and she made it clear that she knew what was best for her children. As a result, a white man was the preferred choice of husband for her daughters. After my mother's older sister, jilted Graham, was he the obvious choice as a husband for her? But my mother had to obey her mother's wishes and bore nine children, some fair-skinned with straight hair and some very dark-skinned with coarse and bushy hair. I never questioned my identity. I just accepted that I have darker skin and different hair than some of my siblings.

Annie openly accepted the older, fairer siblings, while the dark-skinned children were outcasts. My other aunts followed the family line by marrying and bearing white children, making my grandmother very proud. Those were the favoured ones who eventually inherited her wealth.

APARTHEID

APARTHEID SHAPED MY WAY OF being. The label "coloured" was synonymous with being sub-standard, mediocre, not worthy and not good enough to be socially acceptable. This word, now entrenched in the English language, encapsulated the white colonialist minority's dominance over the mixed and black people of South Africa.

The Prohibition of the Mixed Marriages Act No 55 of 1949 was promulgated to create a time when love across the colour barrier was a crime.

Society at the time made us believe that love across the colour divide was a tragedy and being born from such a union was shameful, dirty and wrong. We were the stark physical evidence of defying the government and its laws by lusting and loving across the colour line. White was synonymous with purity. It was clean and acceptable, while mixed-race was considered dirty, a shame, and thus undeserving of acceptance.

I remember when I was about ten, my sisters had European boyfriends, and we were regularly raided by the police trying to catch them together. My sisters had to leave home as it became too dangerous to be with their boyfriends. The rumours of people going missing were constantly circulating. In those days, we were unaware of human rights, either at home or abroad; we accepted the way things were.

Your skin colour determined your social standing; White skin was a passport to privileges and wealth. Mixed-race people had limited access to benefits and prosperity, and black people had almost no access. Being born in a deeply divided country with the government's policy of keeping people of different races apart was the biggest obstacle for me to overcome to succeed.

My sister Pat, who has white skin, straight black hair, and a prominent nose, could easily pass for "white".

Her most significant achievement in life was marrying an Austrian man, giving her an air of superiority. I was not allowed to visit them unless I wore a maid's uniform and pretended to work for them, to avoid being prosecuted by the police.

MANDELA

NELSON MANDELA WAS STILL ON trial for treason the year I was born. However, we were completely unaware of his existence. The first time I heard about Mandela was during the 1976 riots. Still, news about him was minimal since we didn't have TV and the apartheid government didn't broadcast any information about apartheid.

The Western Cape was predominantly made up of people of colour, scattered around the city fringes. The Group Areas Act ensured that Grassy Park, Retreat and Steenberg were among those suburbs designated for "second class citizens". Not black, but certainly not white!

One of the tragedies of apartheid was the ingrained belief system of the Afrikaner that anyone without white skin was inferior. They justified their attitude and segregation policies by quoting their Bible passages. It was a time when the majority of South Africans had lost all dignity and self-esteem. The consequence of marriage across the racial divide was a criminal offence resulting in jail, torture and, for a few, death once incarcerated.

"WHITES ONLY" placards adorned our parks, benches, railway carriages, beaches, restaurants, schools and hospitals. The extremists in this culture called themselves the Broederbond (roughly translated as the Brotherhood). During the period when government employees were sworn to the ideological commitment of separatism, the electoral system forbade non-whites to vote.

PARENTS

I WAS THE SEVENTH CHILD of nine children, given the names Elizabeth Ulrica (Elizabeth, meaning consecrated to God, and Ulrica meaning leader of all). The duality of these two personalities cohabiting in one body has unknowingly shaped who I am and guided my relentless pursuit to find my true purpose in life.

It seemed that the universe cushioned me through my harsh formative years until I was strong enough to cope. While growing up believing that Elizabeth, Eureka, was my name, it was only when I applied for my official identity document that I discovered my legal registered name is Ulrica.

Socially I remained Liz but, characteristically, I had unconsciously been living the personality of Ulrica (a German name), meaning a leader who doesn't tolerate anything but being the best.

Graham, my father, was not only a handsome man with black hair and gentle blue eyes, but he was also a caring, hardworking, and family-oriented parent. Graham had to reclassify from white to coloured to live as a typical family, as you could never be classified up but could move down. My father worked as a boilermaker at the Simonstown Naval Base. I always enjoyed our annual trip to the open day to see where he spent most of his days. Despite the growing number of children in our house, he always provided for us, and we never went to bed hungry.

Apart from their early years of sexual activity, my parents were not an average married couple who shared the same bed. On the contrary, the house was always overfilled with people, creating an atmosphere of dysfunction and mild chaos. But, in their defence, my parents were indeed not unique. There was an undercurrent of turmoil and anger resulting from apartheid regulations changing the psyche of families desperate to find their place in an abnormal new society.

Our family exploded with children in an era when sex education was non-existent, contraceptives were not available, and there was no television to keep people occupied. Parental support for children was lacking, and little attention was paid to individual development. It was survival of the fittest when growing up and progressing through life, for my siblings and I were tough. It was a time of shame and guilt.

Behavioural patterns change when you are outcast and relegated to a lower-class area.

I recall my grandmother Annie sitting in the black limousine behind her chauffeur outside the house on Military Road. She never entered our humble home but summoned my mother to go outside and talk to her.

Maria, my mother, was a beautiful woman, in spite of her cleft palate, she was a feisty and fun-loving woman with soft, shoulder-length black curls framing her face. Yet, it was her eyes that struck the greatest note as they displayed an inner strength and determination. She was an extremely proud person and didn't show any vulnerability. In spite of her cheerful appearance, she was an indomitable fighting force, ensuring the survival of her family.

Besides being a part-time housekeeper for wealthy homes in Constantia, she was also a true entrepreneur. She found many ways to generate extra money by making sweet treats like fudge, coconut ice and toffee apples sold from the house to the many children living in the area.

SEWING AND DESIGNING

MY MOTHER WAS CLEVER WITH her hands and could knit and sew remarkably well, to the point where most of the children's clothing was homemade. I learnt some of these skills from my mother and enjoyed helping her knit jerseys and caps for her family.

With the first Barbie doll I received, I was in my element, designing and sewing the most beautiful clothes from my mother's offcuts. Before that, my constant companions were my paper dolls, cut from the pages of old magazines.

Times were tough, and politics forced everyone to make decisions that were not natural. Families were divided, with the better-educated families choosing to emigrate to where their children would have a fighting chance at everyday life

Our humble, modest house in Military Road boasted a tall tree in the garden that would play a part in bucking the system during the 1976 riots. The elevated position allowed the rioters to throw stones at the police cars, then duck into the house for safe cover. The house had three bedrooms, an add-on room and an outside toilet. The garden was the usual Cape Flats dust bowl, made up of dirty sand deposited millions of years ago when the area was underwater. Playing in the garden meant adding another layer of grime that was only removed on bath days.

Ebrahims' butchery and supermarket were across the busy main road. Navigating my way to the shop often posed the risk of being run over by fast oncoming traffic. It was the main thoroughfare to the white areas across the railway line.

Despite the separation from wealthier suburbs, the view of Elephant's Eye Mountain from our treetop was spectacular. The eye was a vast cave used in ancient times as a portal, facing east, welcoming the rising sun. From the top of the tree, where I often cocooned myself, I could see the whole world and dream of a promising future in faraway places. Luckily, no high-rise buildings blocked my view, giving me equal access to a God-given gift that no government could destroy in my imagination. Our proximity to the sea allowed families to fish, which helped put food on the table. Fresh fish of the day was sold from bakkies parked on the corner on Military Road. Fresh fruit and vegetables were bought on weekly credit from the merchant on his donkey cart.

I loved exploring the several hidden caves in the mountain. We took many walks, especially when we vowed to find the treasure at the end of the rainbow, which led us to the top. I first went to the top of Table Mountain when I met Rudi, who became a scoutmaster, and I regularly accompanied them on their mountain hikes. Hiking remains one of my passions – along with dancing - to this day.

STOMPING GROUNDS

THESE STOMPING GROUNDS WERE MY reality, shared with eight siblings for the foreseeable future. My younger sister Cat and I shared the front bedroom with my mother, all sleeping on a double bed until Ava, my youngest sister, arrived. After that, I was relegated to a mattress on the floor in the "girls" room where Pat, Fran and Felicia shared a double bed. While my mother gave birth to Ava, Pat was pregnant with her first child, followed by a second who shared the same space as us.

Finally, the boys and my father shared the third room, except when it was rented out to a boarder to help pay towards the household expenses. They would then move to the add-on room in the backyard. There was a hierarchy in the house based solely on money earned for the family, leaving the balance of children to be skivvies, cleaning, cooking and fetching for those who made money.

Being two years apart, Cat and I became very close. We played together and shared the same passion for creating beautiful clothes for our paper or cloth dolls. Unfortunately, she was a stutterer and had difficulty pronouncing my name. She referred to me as "Libbet", which became my name amongst my family and friends to this day.

Before school, part of my morning chores was to empty the pee pot that the girls used during the night. Unfortunately, in a rush to get through my duties, which included serving tea to my mother in bed, and making it in time for school, I sometimes spilled some pee on the floor. As a result, I bore the brunt of her anger—many days running without combing my bushy hair if I had overslept.

For those who take toilet paper for granted, you should know that completing the ablutions with newspaper means sharp edges and smeared soiled cheeks and clothing. The evening wash was conducted in a small bath with hot water, where I rubbed my feet together. The proper bath took place on Sunday evening, after pots of water had been boiled on the coal stove all afternoon. Finally, my tangled, bushy hair was washed, after having endured hours of excruciating pain as my older sisters searched for lice, despite my fierce protest and frustrated tears.

For most people of colour, hair was something we struggled with in our households and the community. Our curly or wavy hair was frowned upon. We would straighten it out by placing our hair on a flat surface, covering our curls with brown paper and using a warm or hot iron. Then, the magical "swirl kous" was discovered, made from laddered pantyhose. To keep our hair straight and intact while we slept, we would cut off one leg, knot the end (foot), and pull it tight over our carefully brushed hair. I found this to be the perfect solution for my unruly curly hair, and it made my life so much simpler, and the "swirl kous" became a night time staple for girls and boys obsessed with having straight hair. The women carried one in their bags, while the men kept one in their pockets for fear of losing it.

TVs were relatively new in SA at the time, and we were one of the first families to own one in our neighbourhood. So "Peter en Heidi" was the first series we watched on TV after listening to stories on the radio.

I knew of wealth only through the babbis, a slang term used to describe an Indian shopkeeper across the street. I used to wait in long lines for hours to be attended to, while white people and adults received priority, even though I had arrived first. This persistent "conscious bias" built up a silent rage within me.

Insight:

Love is the energy of our Soul, and its purpose is to achieve self-love and thus Enlightenment. A Soul will inhabit a physical body, in our case, a human body. Whether black, white or brown, it is the appropriate colour to physically experience and learn or continue lessons from a previous lifetime on earth.

These lessons, such as self-respect, self-acceptance, self-worth and others, are all aspects of self-love to attain the ultimate goal of Enlightenment.

The Soul chooses parents and siblings who are at a similar level on the continuum of self-love. They will be the first mentors/teachers on our path to remind us of our purpose. Wherever the parents are on this spectrum, whether it's at the stage of low self-esteem, self-loathing, or any aspects of the above, their child will learn this way of being. That will then be the lesson the Soul came to the physical plane to transcend to get to the next level.

Children do not learn through words but through emotions, which is the language of the Soul. A person's Soul absorbs the energy vibration of their parents and siblings, which then becomes their foundation for developing and growing.

CHILDHOOD

LEO WAS MY OLDER BROTHER by ten months, and we attended the Moravian church school together, which was a five-minute walk through a patch of bush.

I remember running through the bush with my thin scraggy legs on enormous feet without shoes and wild, uncombed hair. I wore my red coat almost every day to school, no matter the weather. I only started wearing proper shoes in Standard Two. Since most of the children at school walked barefoot, I never felt out of place.

Our school's modest face-brick building seemed out of place amongst the dunes; it was painted a creamy-white and rust-brown to absorb dirt. In addition, the asbestos roof resulted in a suicidal heat that made it impossible for students to concentrate.

As it was close to Muizenberg beach, one of the windiest areas in the Cape, dunes became our playground with a constant struggle to flatten the dunes that would build up overnight.

My reputation as the stinky girl caused me to be shunned, and no one wanted to be my friend during the first two years at school. My breaks were spent sitting alone behind the school building, enduring the constant onslaught of the wind blowing sand into my eyes, mouth and hair.

I was too shy to ask my teacher if I could go to the toilet, so I wet myself in class almost every day for the first year of school. Leo was then summoned to clean the bench and puddle on the floor from his classroom. Leo never forgave me for the humiliation he had to endure. He bullied and tormented me well after my teenage years.

At six, I found solace in the local library after school, which was only three blocks away from our house. This unassuming little face brick building became my quiet haven for learning. A window into the world of possibilities and a secret hide-away enabling me to escape into mystical realms where pixies and fairies were very real. I loved reading about witches, fairies, fantasy, and borrowers (miniature humans) that lived in the forest. They fascinated me and I hunted for them when we were in the forest.

Despite my age, I felt a strong sense of being different from my family during those moments of introspection. My personality didn't always resonate with the group, and I felt detached, like an outsider, which caused me to feel incredibly lonely and sad. The hollow feeling of being a separate entity remained with me, since I could not quite articulate it or discuss it with anyone without sounding like a nutcase. So, I started pretending to be someone people wanted to be around to fit in, especially with my sisters and the girls at school. To entertain my older sisters, I would put on one of my sister's nightgowns and impersonate celebrities like Conni Francis. I became a chameleon.

From this early age, I have had an affinity for birds. I remember how thrilled I was when my brother caught and brought home pigeons. I felt a bond with the pigeons and, throughout my life, birds would comfort me whenever I was in turmoil. However, I only realised the total value of this phenomenon later in life as I became more spiritually aware.

My father would leave home at 6am to travel to Simonstown, arriving home after 6pm, exhausted and hungry. Soon my mother would serve supper. After that, my father would help clean the kitchen. He would then retire to the lounge to read the newspaper or slump in a chair until bedtime.

On the other hand, I had an Uncle John, a tall, charming man with dark skin, who was a close friend of my mother. Even though he was much younger than my mother, they seemed to have a special bond as she laughed a lot when he was around. He always seemed happy to see me, laughing and throwing me up into the air and then catching me and carrying me on his shoulders, calling me his princess.

Then there were Aunty Rosie, Uncle John's sister, and her husband. They owned a garage and were considered to be rich in the community. I shared treat days with Jean, who was my age, and her Ouma (grandmother), who was the caretaker at the public toilets in Kalk Bay. Picnics below the railway line in the fishing harbour included luxuries we had never seen in our house. She brought old cake (past its sell-by date), kaaings - excess batter from the fish and chip shop - French Polony and peanut butter in her basket.

The main harbour in the southern suburbs was Kalk Bay, where we could buy fresh fish, and people mixed freely, regardless of race. The hardworking, honest fishermen were paid a fair price for their catch. Bright green, blue and red fishing boats chugged in and out of the harbour, leaving at "sparrows" and returning with their catch at about five in the afternoon. The fishermen would display the cob, yellowtail and snoek in order of price, waiting for the locals to bargain with them. The fish usually became cheaper the closer we got to the cleaning cubicle because white buyers didn't like the smell of Dettol.

At the age of seven, I started to black out at school. Any exertion would send me into a dizzy spin, leaving the local doctors confused and worried. Because we didn't have a family car, my mother and I travelled part of the time on foot and on the train to the children's Red Cross Hospital.

A series of tests revealed a blockage in my heart, and I spent my eighth birthday in hospital. The hospital was nice enough, and the nurses were friendly. I shared a room with a little black boy who became my friend. The thought of dying never crossed my mind, so I did not fear the operation as I felt it needed to be fixed. Dr. Chris Barnard performed my open-heart surgery. Later that year, he performed the first heart transplant at Groote Schuur Hospital. He was a very gentle and kind man, and I had no idea he was a famous doctor.

I endured being bullied at school by one particular girl. I was afraid to tell my mother about this in case she came to school to confront the girl. I was scared that I'd be victimised even more. One day, during the break, the girl attacked me and made fun of me in front of the other children so I retaliated. This girl challenged me to a physical fight after school. I had no choice but to accept the challenge, although I was dreading the end of the school day. I couldn't concentrate in class because I was so nervous. Since I had never physically fought with a big child, I felt I had to save face, even though I was scared.

Once I arrived at the agreed spot, ready for the fight, I found she had run home as soon as school ended. Giddy with relief, I walked home feeling like I had won the Olympics. I learned that if you stand up to a bully, they will invariably cave in. Bullies hate being bullied, so she never teased me again. I realised that I dared to stand up for myself for the first time in my life. A fighter was born, a strength born of deep anger that I used constructively throughout my life. I even started protecting my little sisters when the neighbourhood children picked on them.

Insight:

During our first six years of life, our parents, siblings and the environment profoundly influence us, resulting in the formation of a "box" of beliefs, consisting of traditions, religion and culture, which is our road to learning and growth. As a result, our thinking, feelings and behaviours are shaped by our beliefs. Unfortunately, most of us get stuck in these limiting beliefs. Unless these are challenged later in life, they will limit our spiritual growth and prevent us from living beyond our "box". The Soul is on a one-way journey towards its ultimate goal and will cross paths with people and face situations that motivate it to move forward.

MOTHER RATIONED HER LOVE

WITH TWO YOUNGER SIBLINGS, I had no chance of getting attention from my mother as a toddler, and I began to believe that my mother didn't love me. I became withdrawn and almost invisible for fear of rejection, not making demands, or asking for anything.

In a house filled with playmates of most ages, you'd assume I would never have felt lonely, but I felt hopelessly unloved, disconnected from the world around me, and yearned for my mother's nurturing without success. My younger sister Cat had become the master manipulator, demanding attention through her rebellious behaviour. She'd throw physical tantrums when my parents went out, demanded the most attention in the house, and bore the brunt of verbal abuse from my older siblings because of it. Because of her dark skin and coarse hair, they dubbed her "Kaffir". I often fought her cause and took on the role of protector, a task I carried well into my adult life. I saw how unhappy my mother was when she acted out this way. I did not want to add to her burden, so I devised another plan to get the love and attention I so desperately craved.

Although I longed for my mother's affection and the odd hug from her, there were always those with more significant needs in the family. My mother was not tactile at all. The way she showed her love was through food, not by touching or even by words. She was an expert at making feasts from the simplest of foods; an egg would become an egg omelette (with onion and chilli), a can of fish with tomatoes, onions and potatoes could feed an army. She demonstrated love for her family this way, and this is exactly how I understood love to be. I believe this led to my eating disorder that started when I was a teenager and followed me into my adult life.

I reasoned that the only way to change the status quo was to be a good child, the best at everything, and the top of the class at school so she could be proud of me and love me.

If I wasn't in the library, I played with cut-out dolls, carefully designed each outfit on white paper, and then coloured it to match the "occasion" or a "fashion show". My favourite subjects in school were history, biology, geography, needlework and accounting, but I hated maths and science.

When I was younger, I dreamt of owning a babbi shop, as they were the only people who were considered wealthy in my community.

A passion for beauty and vibrant colours was slowly taking shape, despite my drab surroundings.

As I grew older, I had this strong desire to help people heal, so I dreamt of becoming a nurse, though part of me was attracted to fabrics and colours. There were always two things I wanted to do at once. I became accustomed to the dualistic nature of my dreams.

FOOD ISSUES

I NEVER HAD A BREAKFAST or lunch box because I lived on the school feeding program, where the government would provide soup on Mondays with a slice of dry brown bread during the week, but on Fridays we would get a treat of peanut butter and bread with a glass of milk Peanut butter sandwiches remain my favourite sandwich of all time. I make sure to pack a jar whenever I travel to a foreign country; it's my lifesaver.

Our food supply at home had usually run out by Friday afternoon, which often left nothing to eat as Leo would have claimed the last piece of bread, leaving nothing for me. Sometimes, I was lucky to find a hard crust and a few grains of sugar. I would spread this thinly across the stale bread with a few drops of water to soften the hard crust. Still, sometimes I would hit the jackpot and find some delicious condensed milk left in the tin. This was a rare treat that I savoured greatly.

The weekly meal consisted of long stews in brown gravy with one vegetable and potatoes, one small piece of meat, and rice per person. Friday night, however, was a treat night with Vienna sausages, eggs and chips for dinner. The weekends were decadent at home, as a case of cold drinks was delivered every Saturday morning, and the younger children received ten cents every week. In those days, the Quiabil Theatre on Retreat main road would sell a movie ticket, chips and a long colourful sweet on a stick for that amount.

During those days, public transportation was scarce, especially on weekends. As a result, we used to walk ten kilometres to the movie theatre with the neighbourhood kids and play cowboys and crooks and hide-and-seek on the way. We would arrive just in time for the movie at noon and then find our way back home just before dusk.

Sunday was my favourite day of the week. My early morning task was to buy the family's breakfast. Then, I would don my red coat, get a large plastic bowl and go around the corner to the Muslim neighbour's house for spicy warm koeksisters. My father would have the tea brewing on the coal stove, and I would serve my sisters and mother koeksisters and tea in bed on my return. After breakfast, the younger children would get ready for Sunday school at the Anglican Church. I attended this church until my early teens, before we changed to become members of the Seventh Day Adventist Church. I listened and learnt all about Jesus and God. I truly believed God was a man in the sky with a big ledger book, who kept score of my good and bad behaviour. A God to be worshipped and feared!

Later, I would help my mother prepare her Sunday feast of roast chicken, curry and rice, while listening to the church service on the radio and singing hymns at the top of her lungs. One of her favourite hymns was "How great thou art".

The best part of the morning was the task of mixing the cake ingredients for the afternoon high tea and then licking the last of the sweet dough left in the bowl. This was a privilege, as my younger siblings all vied for the bowl. I felt very special to be the one who got it most of the time. The time spent with my mother in the kitchen were to become some of my most treasured memories I have of her.

Cake became a symbol of love for me. It is often what I reach for when I feel emotionally "empty". As a child, I was not taught how to cook, and I was not even remotely interested in learning. Cooking is not my strong suit, so I appreciate it when someone prepares meals for me. I do love baking, though.

As each year passed, my school performance improved and I never dropped below third in class. Fran, my older sister, dropped out of school after finishing standard four, taking on the role as an overly strict stepmother who cleaned and polished excessively. She was a firm and very temperamental disciplinarian. I feared her as a child as she showed no mercy. After we had eaten our lunch, consisting of jam and bread, she would toss us out after school to play in the black sand, whether sunshine or rain.

I joined the majority of neighbourhood children playing games in the street after school or catching tadpoles and frogs in the river where broken glass and other trash was thrown by passers-by, resulting in cut feet sometimes requiring stitches. No one was wealthy; drugs were not an issue and the abnormal political landscape was accepted as part of life. These were the happy, carefree days of my childhood.

CHRISTMAS

WE HAD TWO ANOMALIES IN our family behaviour that went against our financial means, but which we could never, in our wildest dreams, accept going without. The first was Christmas, and I'm not referring to the turkey and pudding aspects of it. Regardless of whether we could afford it or not, every Christmas, my parents - like most of the coloured people in our community - would replace all our curtains, which my mother would lay-bye from OK Bazaars or Ackermans on an annual basis.

We painted the house, and everyone was provided with two new sets of clothing, all bought on credit and paid off over six months. The Christmas tree made its appearance from the beginning of December and from then on my mother would start planning the menu. The thought of Christmas approaching made me jump with excitement and anticipation. No expense was spared to provide us with a decadent Christmas experience at our house.

On the 26th of December (Boxing Day), our family would pack up the Christmas leftovers and all the sweet hampers that were paid for by weekly stamps, and we'd set off to the annual camp in Soetwater or Kommetjie for a week.

On one of our camping holidays, I was allowed to take our neighbour's daughter Denise with us. She was one of my closest friends in our neighbourhood and we did everything together. I remember us lying on our backs on the groundsheet of our small tent, gazing up towards the ceiling and dreaming aloud about our future.

I told her, "I'm going to be very wealthy and will fly in private jets one day. I will socialise with the likes of kings and important people and attend very fancy ballroom functions in palaces." My vision was elaborate, and my dreams had no limits. I remember her laughing and saying, "Liz, stop dreaming". In hindsight, everything I dreamt of became a reality.

We would return home the day after New Year so we could go to the annual "coon (*klopse*)" carnival at Athlone stadium. It was an exciting time of the year with Christmas marching bands and the "coons" in our area. Everyone ran outside to watch them, as they proudly marched down the street playing the (*langarm*) songs they'd been practising all year. This was strictly a coloured festival and it reminded me to take pride in my heritage and culture.

The second anomaly was my family's passion for horse racing. Some of us were introduced to this "hobby" at such a young age that gambling became a destructive and addictive theme, but on race day nobody cared. On Saturdays, the entire household was a flurry of pretty dresses and dress suits usually reserved for church. Bradley, my eldest brother, and my father would busily study the horses and their form, gathering tips from the sports section of the Weekend Argus. By 10am, Mom, Dad and Bradley, all dressed smartly, walked to the station to catch the train to Kenilworth racetrack.

There they met with their gambling friends and frittered away some of the household money my father and brother had worked so hard for. This was my family's big weekly entertainment that they looked forward to, where they could be glamorous and feel part of an elite group of people. Winning or losing set the mood for the rest of the week. If the trio arrived home smiling, the household was happy, and if they came home sad, there was an element of gloom.

The first time I was allowed to join my family at the races was at one of the important annual racing events where children were allowed to attend. I wore my best Sunday school dress, which was green with bright flowers, and yellow ribbons in my hair. To add to the excitement, I was allowed to bet on a horse in the main race, called "Sunshine". It seems I was already a sun worshipper then. The thrill of watching my horse win was the perfect hook for an addiction that would last my entire life! After that, I took a keen interest in the horses and started studying their form, as my older brothers had taught me to do.

Another annual highlight of the family was the Klaverjas Ball, usually held at the end of the year in a civic centre in Mitchells Plain. Klaverjas (a four-player trick-taking card game) has now become a national sport because of my father, who was the president of his union and one of the founders. The sport has grown considerably since and many clubs now exist in South Africa, and each has its competitions and prize-giving functions.

My older brothers were also passionate about the game and played for various teams in the province. My parents usually acted as judges and handed out trophies to the winning teams. My mother loved to bask in the admiration from others as she proudly took the stage to present trophies with my father.

When I was a small child, I remember wishing I was old enough to attend these auspicious occasions with my older siblings. I used to get swept up in their excitement weeks before, as they planned their outfits. As one of the most important families at the event, new evening gowns were bought on credit for the occasion

The first time I was allowed to attend the function with my family, I accompanied my mother and my three older sisters to purchase our outfits at Foschini - the posh clothing store where my mother enjoyed VIP status as one of their long-standing customers and we were treated like royalty. My dress, in soft green and gold satin, fitted my sixteen-year-old body like a glove. My hair had been washed and rolled into big green plastic rollers, then sundried for many hours before it was straightened with the hot metal comb. I looked and felt like a princess.

The excitement and exhilaration I felt when I walked into the hall for the first time was a dream come true. There were long tables festively decorated in bright, shimmery colours, candles and fancy flower arrangements. Some guests were enjoying the food platters and sparkling wine, while others were dancing to the orchestra strumming the sounds of our local *Langarm*, or *Sakkie-Sakkie* Afrikaans music. While watching with fascination as beautifully-dressed couples performed the waltz or other type of ballroom dance, I felt like I was watching a movie scene. My parents were professional ballroom dancers as they'd attended the weekly ballroom dance in the Retreat area when they were young adults. It was common for people their age to be able to dance professionally, as it was the only form of dancing they had been exposed to. Onlookers would be mesmerised as they glided effortlessly over the floor like swans on a lake. These are proud memories I cherish to this day.

INFIDELITY

BY NOW WE WERE CONSIDERED fairly comfortable and classy within our community. With a stable, hardworking man in the house, which certainly was not the norm, we were held in high esteem.

My Uncle John often came over when my father was still at work, but I never questioned that as I considered him a family friend, an uncle!

It was only in my teens that I put two and two together and things I had witnessed as a child started to make more sense to me. Then, one day I arrived home after school and froze when I saw my mother and Uncle John kissing passionately! "What are you doing?" I demanded.

"I had something in my eye and John was trying to take it out," she replied, but I knew she was lying.

Blindly, I ran out of my house, not knowing where I was going, but kept running until I eventually stopped at a public park where I collapsed on the grass and burst into tears. I was shocked by what I had just witnessed. The scene kept playing itself out over and over in my head. "How could they do this to me?" I kept asking myself as feelings of anger, disgust and betrayal consumed me. "I can't wait to tell my father when he gets home," I promised myself, and that's exactly what I did. I blurted out the incident as soon as he stepped into the door. Visibly shaken he stayed calm but, unbeknown to us, he banned Uncle John from the house. I believe he had already known about the affair.

I made up my mind that sex was a dirty and shameful act and cried every time I saw one of my older sisters kiss their boyfriends until my teenage years.

Almost twenty years passed before I saw Uncle John again.

My mother was very angry with me, and my older siblings blamed me for causing trouble in the family. The toxic atmosphere caused me to want to leave home, so I went to live with Aunty Rosie, although I cried the entire night and went back home the following day.

Nothing more was said about the "scandal" and everyone went about their daily lives as normal. However, for a while, I was an outcast in the house and no one would acknowledge or engage with me.

I learnt that certain things are best left unspoken and that I should accept the way things are. It left me with the sense that my feelings or opinions were not valid and that it's best not to speak the truth for fear of losing my family's love and approval.

I'm not sure if this is where I made the subconscious decision not to "feel" anymore, but I made a vow to myself that I would never give anyone the power to hurt me again. So, from then on I showed no emotion, taking my beatings at school until I could not sit on my bum or use my hand to write, but I showed no sign of pain. Even when my mother beat me with the washing machine hosepipe, I never showed any sign that I was hurt, and this made her punish me even more. I had successfully blocked out my pain.

I think it was around that time that I started using food as my crutch by eating up my emotions. Food became an obsession to the point of stealing food stored in the oven overnight when everyone was sleeping. I was insatiable and there just was never enough!

EATING DISORDER

HIGH SCHOOL STARTED WITH A whimper rather than a bang for me. By this stage, I had grown into a young woman. I had developed large breasts. However, one was visibly larger than the other due to the scar from my heart operation, which I found embarrassing, and although I tried to hide my breasts under oversized clothing, I only had one school uniform which was becoming far too small, and my shirt buttons started to take strain.

I finally found the courage to tell my mother about my maths teacher after he tried to grope me several times. To my astonishment, instead of confronting the lecherous teacher, she swiftly whipped me out of the school and enrolled me at Heathfield High, which was perceived to be a classier school and much more fun. Heathfield allowed me the opportunity to hone my competitive edge in academic subjects. Initially, my play-breaks consisted of "alone time", sitting on the grass, dreaming of a prosperous future. Then I gradually made new friends who, luckily, included me in their inner circle. I became part of the "popular girls group" and suddenly I experienced being popular, something I had never known.

From years of eating rationed food that had no second helpings, I had developed an eating disorder. I binged on stolen food at night, and then put my fingers down my throat to chuck it all up in the outside toilet where no one could hear me. My anxiety and striving to be perfect probably triggered the bulimia. Chocolates and cake bought from the school tuck shop with my bus fare simply replaced my mother's love.

I didn't realise that bingeing was seen as a disorder. It was more of a shameful habit that I lived with and that I never discussed with anyone. Nobody had even heard of Bulimia then, and we didn't know anything about eating disorders. It wasn't common in my family or the community.

KNITTING MACHINE

AT THE TENDER AGE OF fourteen, a saviour arrived in the form of a fancy knitting machine that my mother bought on credit.

I was forced to learn to use the machine to earn extra money for the family. With patience and drive, I practised on the machine and taught myself by trial and error, often after having to knit the same jersey several times over by unravelling it, until it was finally the size the customer ordered. This often meant I had to knit all through the night to complete an order for collection the following day. Homework was only looked over at 5am and, for the first time in my life, I experienced academic failure. When my Standard 7 report read "Failed" there was a sense of stunned disbelief. Failure for me was a fate worse than death!

I realised I had to work much harder to pass, as well as fill all the knitting orders that were streaming in from factories in the area. An outsider might have suggested that I put school first and hand over the reins to other members of the family, but this was simply not an option, as my sisters hadn't mastered the machine as I had. My sudden drop in grades at school was a direct result of my working too hard. There was just no time at all to study or do homework.

For the first time in my life, I was the top earner in the household, the queen of supply, and my mother's darling. Success tasted good. I felt powerful, exhilarated. Suddenly, I could command respect! Despite the demands on my time, I came seventh out of the forty-five children in my class at the end of the year. For the next two years, I was showered with new clothes which included blue denim jeans and a watch for my sixteenth birthday, a token of appreciation from my mother, but my wish to attend college or university was never discussed. My hard-earned money was allocated instead towards my brother Leo's university fees.

Tertiary education was reserved for men and the rest of the family gratefully participated in the launch of their career paths. By contrast, I was expected to find a job and get married, preferably to someone with a decent bank balance, sooner rather than later. There was resignation or a level of acceptance that bore little animosity to this situation because this was the norm. It was still a man's world, never to be questioned.

Gradually, I built my confidence and developed a personality. I was an immensely proud but aloof girl, with emotions firmly intact. My admirers and circle of friends grew in proportion to the rebel traits I displayed.

I had a teenage crush on a boy I saw on the bus in the mornings, but it never occurred to me to want to be with him as I knew being "with someone" only happened once I was married. I never actually spoke to him personally. I wasn't looking for a boyfriend, though. My dream was to go to college and become a nurse or a dress designer. I chose the only available option, which was to attend the dress designing college in Wynberg, where I studied part-time in the evenings.

When I finally discovered the disco, I only ever wanted to dance. I became a professional flirt. I knew instinctively that I could get any boy if I wanted to, but I wasn't interested in marriage or relationships. It was just the hunt that was exciting for me at that stage of my life. Once a boy was interested, I lost interest in him.

DIVINE INTERVENTION

As a sixteen-year-old, I had never been to a disco before as my mother was very protective of us. Because I was one of the highest earners in the family, she agreed that I could join my two school friends for a matinee disco in Wynberg one Saturday afternoon. Happy with the way I looked, in my new jeans and green striped cotton shirt, together with my hard-earned new watch, I proudly set off to the station to catch the train to Wynberg, excited to meet everybody at 4pm. When I got to the station earlier than 4pm, I started to pace up and down waiting for my friends. A frustrating two hours passed with no friend in sight and sunlight was turning to dusk. I started to feel uneasy and climbed on the next train heading back to Steenberg, arriving around 7pm when dusk had turned to darkness.

The brisk walk home at this hour was dangerous, down a long road sandwiched between bushes, the perfect hideout for boys up to no good. I saw three of them at the top of the road, running towards me, and realised that, no matter what their intentions, I would never get away so decided to keep walking with an air of confidence. They were running head-on towards me and, when one grabbed me from behind, I caught the glint of the bread knife under the moonlight that one of the guys pressed against my throat. My throat was slightly grazed by it, but I didn't get cut or draw blood.

The others grabbed my arms and closed my mouth as they started pulling me into the bushes. Terrified, I begged, "Please don't hurt me. You can take my watch, my new shirt, jeans and shoes. I will even give you money if you come home with me," I pleaded, but they weren't listening.

"Shut up," one of them shouted, as they starting pulling me into the bush.

"Please help me, God. I promise to be good from now on," I bargained with God.

Suddenly, out of nowhere a crowd of people came running down the road towards me shouting, as apparently these guys had just robbed someone down the road. My three assailants dropped me and fled into the bushes. Relieved and thankful, I ran home and did not share the incident with anyone for fear of being put under house arrest for the rest of my teens. This would not be the last time that divine intervention played a part in saving my life!

DINO SUPERMARKET

HAVING SUCCESSFULLY COMPLETED STANDARD 8 (Grade 10), I started to work in the Tokai supermarket for Mr. Dino for R25 per week during the summer holidays. Fran, my older sister who had been interviewed at the same time was rejected and only I was employed, which displeased me as I wanted to go back to school to finish matric.

On my first day at the supermarket, I met a Muslim lady named Fazlin, who was very feisty, sexy and friendly. She ran the entire supermarket and was Mr. Dino's favourite employee. Mr. Dino sat in his office watching over the shop through his one-way glass, while Fazlin and I sat behind the two tills on both sides of the long counter. Fazlin was very confident and all the customers loved her. I felt intimidated at first, but by lunchtime, I had warmed up to her. At 1 pm she asked, "Liz, what would you like to eat for lunch?" This being my first day at the supermarket, I wasn't sure how things worked, so I hesitated and Fazlin went on to ask, "How about an avocado on wholewheat?" Since it was one of my favourites, and Fazlin's as well, I immediately agreed with her choice.

She put R1 (one Rand) coin into my hand. "Go and fetch the avocado and come pay for it at my till," she instructed. With the money she gave me, I got the avocado and paid for it, and she gave me more than R2 change. I stared at her bewilderedly as she ushered me to the kitchen to eat lunch.

Since I was raised in a strict Christian home, my mother taught me not to take anything without her permission. Even opening a tin of beans when I was hungry was forbidden. As I sat there, eating lunch, I realised I had more money than I had ever had. Fazlin carried on with this type of behaviour and I knew that I was caught between exposing Fazlin or accepting things as they were.

At first, I was completely overwhelmed by all the luxuries in the supermarket – delicacies and foods I never knew existed. I was like a child in a toy shop! I wanted to taste everything, especially the sweet stuff. I spent my pocket money buying chocolates, sometimes an entire box that I would hide from the rest of the family and consume all at the same time. I put on an excessive amount of weight and went back to putting my finger down my throat in the toilet, which was my most shameful secret.

Mr. Dino was smitten with Fazlin and whenever he was close to her, he couldn't stop smiling or teasing her. She acted like she owned the shop and had full control over everything. I earned more money daily through Fazlin giving me more change out of her till than my weekly wage of R25. I couldn't tell anyone my secret and didn't know what to do with all the money. I hid the money amongst my clothes in the only drawer I was allocated in our shared wardrobe, and I was very careful when I dressed, since sometimes the money fell out when I removed something from the wardrobe.

For the first time in my life I could buy whatever I desired. Fazlin took me to Wynberg main road to buy new clothing. It felt so good having money; it gave me a sense of freedom and power that I had never had. It was exhilarating.

When the new school year came, my mother told me I couldn't continue my studies and should continue to work at the supermarket as she depended on the money I was earning. I was disappointed as I wanted to study further to become a nurse (it wasn't possible to become a doctor at that time as a non-white). I realised I needed to earn enough money to pay for my studies if I ever wanted to get ahead. My passion for designing clothes continued, but only as a hobby at that stage.

I met many wealthy and influential people who lived in the posh suburbs of Tokai and Constantia and many of the suppliers who delivered fresh produce on an almost daily basis. Amongst these suppliers was Derrick, a young, well-built man who drove a large truck and delivered vegetables and fruit. He had always been friendly and respectful, so over a short period we became friends, chatting about his passion for motorbikes and my ambition to succeed in business. From my point of view, it was an innocent relationship. He sometimes offered me a lift home when he was passing by my house, and I was extremely grateful since I usually walked the 5km to and from work every day.

I was unaware of the attention I was getting from men as I was too focused on getting ahead and excelling in my life. I had many dreams and goals which I wanted to achieve.

CAMPING TRIP

ALTHOUGH I LOVED DANCING AND having fun with my friends, sex was never considered to be something I would take part in until I was married, a belief drilled into me by my mother and my needlework teacher. Easter was approaching and Bradley, my eldest brother, suggested that the family go on holiday to Mossel Bay. The only accommodation we could afford were the tents in the coloured camping site. Diaz Beach was not far away and the Diaz Hotel was nearby so young people could go to discos.

I was surprised when I bumped into Derrick and some of his friends at the camping site. With his black leather boots and padded jacket, he looked quite intimidating, unlike the friendly, easy-going driver whom I was used to seeing in casual work clothes. Derrick invited me, my two sisters and a friend to go with them to the disco at Diaz Hotel that night. I asked my mother, who agreed we could go on the condition that we were back at the camping site by 10pm.

As the bikers arrived at the agreed meeting place, everyone was visibly apprehensive, since we had never ridden on a motorbike before.

Derrick held the helmet out to me. "Here, put this on," he casually commanded, as if I were familiar with helmets and motorbikes. With one lift of his booted leg, he comfortably landed on the seat. "Hop on and hold tight onto me," he instructed as his large frame filled the seat, leaving me with very little space to sit while my arms gripped his leather jacket. I tried to hide my anxiety as this was my first experience on a motorbike which was something I regarded as "death on wheels", after I had witnessed a fatal accident a few years earlier.

In the open air, my nervousness turned into exhilaration, as if I were flying, free as a bird!

After riding in convoy, we arrived at the reception to the blaring sound of disco music. My excitement was palpable and I couldn't wait to hit the dance floor. The group planned to go back to the camping site at 10pm but decided to have a burger at a garage that we had passed on the way. We left together but, when the others slowed down and turned into the garage parking, Derrick accelerated and rode off into the night.

"Where are you going?" I anxiously shouted, my words fading in the wind.

A few minutes later, Derrick stopped the bike on the deserted moonlit Diaz Beach. "Get off," he barked. Panic-stricken, I looked up into his glazed eyes, which had the look of a werewolf. I felt a sense of danger and started shivering with fear and angst.

"Please take me back to my sisters," I begged in a tremulous voice. He didn't hear me. It was as if he were in a trance.

"Take your clothes off," he demanded abruptly as he fiddled with his zipper, but I turned and ran up the beach. With a few long strides he had caught up with me, and punched me hard in my face. As the blood poured from my nose, I saw the flash in his hand. It was a knife, which he held to my throat. "If you do that again, I will kill you," he roared as he tore at my shirt, buttons flying all over the sand he proceeded to drag my unzipped jeans off, pushing me hard onto the sand. As he lunged towards me, I began to hyperventilate, and my body started shaking violently.

"I'm having a heart attack," I stammered.

He suddenly looked up, hesitated for a moment as if he had seen something which changed his mind. 'Get up and get dressed," he shouted hoarsely, as he started pulling his jeans over his knees. "Get on the bike."

A mixture of confusion and relief washed over my body as I struggled to get my clothes on.

When we arrived back at the camping site, I quietly crept into my brother's tent where I blurted everything out to my sister-in-law, who promised not to tell my mother. Derrick and his friends must have left the camp very early as I never saw him again after that incident.

At no time during my many interactions with Derrick did I pick up that he wanted more than a friendship. He never gave me that impression and I certainly didn't see him as anything more than an acquaintance. He had never tried to be intimate with me before. I continued working for Mr. Dino for a few months after the incident but never saw Derrick again.

I could no longer live with the dishonesty and the betrayal of stealing from a kind and generous man whom I'd learned to care about and so left my job. I got the opportunity many years later to absolve myself when Mr. Dino came to purchase curtains at my establishment and I gave him an unusually large discount.

Insight:
Derrick saw something which made him change his mind. I remember him looking up into the distance before suddenly demanding that I get up and get dressed! I do believe it was divine intervention, because he was lost in that moment of madness, and rational thought was far from that crazy, demonic mood he was in.

I could not understand why he did not rape or assault me as was his intention. I was left with a deep sense of gratitude and a knowing that some higher power had saved me. Throughout my childhood and teenage years I was aware that I had a higher purpose. This realisation was brought home with so many strange things that happened to me and messages I was receiving. I never shared these feelings with anyone as I did not understand them. For me it was normal, and I thought that everyone experienced this, but as I got older I started feeling very lonely and separate from my siblings and friends.

RUDI

MY BROTHER LEO, WHO WAS studying at Western Cape University, had made many friends from the surrounding areas: some from very impoverished backgrounds, others more privileged. Every so often, they would drop by, attracted to our household by several good-looking sisters.

One Saturday evening, when I was under house arrest and watching TV with my parents as most of my siblings were out, I heard a loud knock on the door. I wasn't expecting anyone in particular, so I casually opened the door. I was surprised to see a tall man wearing jeans tucked into cowboy boots on the doorstep. "I'm Rudi. Is Leo home?" he inquired in an unusually loud voice.

"Come inside," I invited, as I called my brother and left him to speak to my parents. Within minutes he had won my parents over and I heard laughter coming from the lounge.

Rudi was smitten the moment he laid eyes on me. He was a good-looking man with green eyes with an air of self-assurance that bordered on arrogance. From the day he met me he couldn't stay away. He visited daily and even though I was not that interested in him romantically, he kept on pursuing me. He was a very persuasive and charming man and I eventually succumbed to his pressure and agreed to date him. When he pulled up outside our house with his fancy sunglasses and open sports car, the neighbours would come outside to stare at this man who did not belong in our neighbourhood. I was the envy of all the young women in the area, including some of my white cousins.

He showered me with gifts and took me to many interesting places. One night he told me to dress up as he was taking me to a restaurant. I had never been to a restaurant where people were served at the table. I'd only ever had take-away food, as restaurants were reserved for white people only.

As we entered the restaurant, I felt very self-conscious because every white person seated was staring at us as if we were aliens. Rudi asked for a table and we were shown to a table by a waitress who was clearly unsure if she was doing the right thing. While waiting for a menu, the manager came over to ask us to leave as we were not welcome there, pointing towards a sign on the door which read, "Whites only". A wave of shame and humiliation washed over me as we were led to the exit. The discrimination confirmed that I was not "good enough" and the anger which followed consumed me.

Rudi quickly became part of the family and stole the heart of my parents who accepted him, even though he was Muslim, though as a Christian the possibility of marrying out of my faith was not a consideration.

Our courtship stretched out over six months and he became more and more sexually demanding. Eventually, I gave in to the constant pressure and submitted to his demands, as I felt obligated to repay all of the gifts and money he had lavished on me. This was a very serious "sin" in my life that I could not share with anyone.

The persistent sexual demands made by Rudi and my fear of my mother finding out led me to cry for help most drastically and destructively. I took an overdose of tablets, which landed me in the emergency room at Groote Schuur Hospital, where I had my stomach pumped by disapproving medical staff. I was too ashamed that anyone - especially my mother - would find out that I'd committed the ultimate sin by having sex before marriage. I would rather die than be seen or branded as a cheap slut. I did not intend to kill myself; it was more of a cry for help.

When my mother discovered we were having a sexual relationship, she confronted Rudi. "So, what are your intentions with my daughter?" she asked.

"I'm going to marry her," Rudi replied. I was only seventeen and not ready to marry anyone, but I knew that I had no choice but to marry Rudi, otherwise I would be labelled a "bad girl". The belief that sex was reserved only for marriage forced me into this union. For me, the most important motivating factor was that somebody loved me!

Sleeping together at my parents' house was incredibly stressful. I did so only to please him. Therefore, I attempted suicide. It wasn't that he was cold, but that he was demanding.

I was resigned to the fact that I couldn't fight his obsession but instead had to accept what was happening to me in my life. The fact that he showered me with gifts made me feel very obligated towards him and I felt I owed him something, so we started having sex before the marriage.

Rudi didn't propose to me in the traditional way, down on one knee clutching a ring. I gave him the ultimatum and he agreed. I think if our parents had not interfered and demanded we marry, it would not have happened. However, with hindsight, everything that happened was supposed to.

RUDI'S PARENTS

WHEN RUDI'S PARENTS DISCOVERED THAT their son was seeing a Christian girl, they decided to visit my family at our council house and clear the air. As a result of many discussions, our parents decided that we should get married and the 16th of December was set as the wedding date. Before we could marry, I had to attend Muslim school and convert to Islam. I was taken to a woman who lived in the area who performed circumcision on females. At the age of 18 and having to convert to Islam, the traditions were confusing and completely strange to me, but I accepted this as part of my new life. It seemed to me like it was common practice. My name was changed to Nazlie, which I had difficulty adjusting to, although my family and friends continued to call me "Liz".

I was in deep turmoil; all my dreams of becoming someone important had been shattered. I was scared of the future, of leaving my family and home, of having to adapt to a different culture. However, I knew I couldn't pull out for fear of being branded as a "slut", since I thought of girls who slept with men before marriage as "sluts".

The first time I visited Rudi's home during the courtship was a frightening experience as I was in awe of his father from the moment I met him. He was a big, intimidating man who dwarfed even his son, who was already taller than average. He was a no-nonsense man and anyone who dared to cross him was lucky if he lived to tell the tale. He seemed fearless! He lived by his own rules and those who did not agree with him bore the brunt of his aggression. Rudi was terrified of his father and feared his wrath.

The day before our wedding was arranged to take place, Rudi's father decided on a whim that he no longer wanted his son to marry and cancelled the wedding plans. I was furious and insulted at his arrogance and disregard for all the efforts my mother had put into this big event. She had baked for hours and got the neighbours and family involved, and they went all out to make this a special day for me.

I gave Rudi an ultimatum: "We marry or we break up". He agreed to marry me, and on our way out we stole the freshly baked chocolate cake in his mother's kitchen and booked into the Holiday Inn, in Woodstock, where we spent a pre-honeymoon night. The following day we got married in front of the local Sheikh in Salt River, with a small celebration held at our family home with me wearing a dress borrowed from my sister. After the wedding celebration, Rudi went home to his parents and I continued to live with my family. I gave in to the direction my life had taken. I felt like I was in a trance, like a robot, obeying everything that crossed my path without question. It was as if I had died along with my dreams.

As a result of his father's arrogance, I only considered marriage as a battle of wills. I never really wanted to marry Rudi or anyone else at that time in my life. I was not in love with him; in fact, I was extremely intimidated and afraid of him.

My dream of having a white wedding only came true later in life.

Life went on as normal while Rudi was at varsity. By this time I had moved on from the supermarket and was now working with my older siblings at Plessey, working a night shift and knitting on the machine during the day.

Rudi had bought me a small blue Volkswagen on a five-year loan agreement through the bank, paying the instalments from his monthly allowance from his parents. My parents decided to sell their house in Steenberg to move to Mitchells Plain, a suburb created for Coloured people by the apartheid government which was off the beaten track, where public transport was non-existent and I needed the car to travel to work.

CAR CRASH

A FEW DAYS AFTER OUR move I returned to work with my older brother Jeff, as we were both working the same shift. Fran and my mother wanted a lift to visit friends in Steenberg. I was now more confident behind the wheel but was not ready to do my driver's licence test yet. We were chatting and in good spirits. As I was driving along Baden Powel Drive suddenly, out of nowhere, a stray dog ran across the road. Instinctively I put my foot hard on the brakes to avoid hitting the dog, causing the car to swerve violently on the loose gravel on the side of the road and then everything spun out of control. I must have blacked out for several minutes because, when I awoke, I was upside down as the car had overturned and was lying on its roof.

Disoriented and dazed, I looked around me and saw my brother Jeff lying on the passenger seat, my mother crumpled on the back seat, but Fran was nowhere to be seen. She had been thrown out of the back window and was lying in the nearby bushes. As I struggled to get out of my driver's window, unsteady and in shock, some passers-by had already notified the hospital of the accident. The ambulance arrived and Fran, who had broken her right arm in a few places, was put on a stretcher. My mother had broken a rib and Jeff had some minor injuries. Although I was not injured beyond a minor concussion, a scratch wound on my arm, and a bruised ego, the thought that I was responsible for my family's pain consumed me. I felt terrible that I had been spared.

Unfortunately, the car was a write-off and, because I did not have a driver's licence, we couldn't claim from the insurance. Rudi tried to get a false license from one of his father's friends - who was a police officer - but that failed when the police officer in question committed suicide. We resigned ourselves to the fact that we would have to pay the balance of the car off over the 5-year term. A month later, though, when Rudi dutifully made his usual payment to the bank, he was notified that the insurance had already settled the car and his money was returned.

Insight:
My gratitude was not as great this time; instead, I wished I had been in the hospital instead of Fran.

We were both overjoyed and immensely grateful for this miracle!

ABUSE

RUDI'S PARENTS DISCOVERED THAT WE were married a few months later and persuaded me to go and live with them. My only choice was to share Rudi's room and to adapt to life in a foreign culture and family. I was nervous, afraid and desperately wanted to fit into my new life.

After a while of doing nothing, I decided to study further and went to evening classes at a local high school. I went back to work for Tokai supermarket and whilst on the contraceptives I fell pregnant with my first child.

I was shocked at the news as it came as a surprise, but abortion was not an option. I accepted and carried on with my studies but left my job. When I was three months pregnant, I had a fight with Rudi which turned physical when he hit me in the face with a shoe. That was my first encounter with physical abuse at the hands of my husband. I cried hysterically and ran downstairs to complain to his mother, but was stunned at her casual reaction. She looked at me with a sneer, saying, "So?" with sarcastic humour. This had never happened in our house before, so I was shocked. My father was the epitome of gentlemanliness, never shouting or swearing; only punishing his children under duress when my mother demanded he discipline us.

By rationalising the abuse, I told myself that I must have angered him and that I deserved the punishment. After all, he loved me and would never intentionally harm me, would he? I believed not

I was so surprised and disappointed at his mother's reaction. I'd never witnessed abuse in our home between my parents and was shocked when it happened.

Initially, I was intimidated by Rudi's mother's business demeanour, but I quickly developed a deep admiration for her. After the incident, I had far less respect for her. My mother was the matriarch in the family and I considered her a strong woman. When I met my mother-in-law and saw the abuse she tolerated at the hands of her husband, I lost any respect I had for her, and it was only with hindsight that I saw how much she had sacrificed for her marriage.

It wasn't until I walked in her shoes with her son that I realised how courageous and practical she was, since that's how I dealt with Rudi. It was easier to have him in my life to help care for my children than to struggle to raise them on my own while running a large company.

We can so easily judge if we aren't in the same position as the other person.

PREGNANCY

UPON HEARING ABOUT THE PHYSICAL abuse, my mother brought me home and graciously allowed me to sleep on the couch cushions on the lounge floor, in their new home in Mitchells Plain. It was there that I stayed until after my son was born. With great excitement, my mother and I knitted caps, booties and jackets in neutral colours for my unborn baby, not knowing the gender of the baby. Every time we finished an outfit, I would proudly pack up the baby's few pieces of clothing I'd made from offcuts my mother bought at the town centre - although this time it was not for my Barbie, but my firstborn child. I was impatiently waiting for him or her to arrive.

Having undergone a heart operation, I was required to attend antenatal sessions at Groote Schuur hospital.

Mitchells Plain was a relatively new area with a weak transport network, so this was no ordinary routine visit. We started at 5am, walked to the Town Centre, took a taxi to Mannenberg, changed into a taxi to Mowbray and took a train to Observatory, then walked up the hill to Groote Schuur Hospital, where we arrived at 8am. We would then begin the long exhausting journey home, arriving at 7pm.

Although Rudi had a car, he never came to visit me or offered to take me to the hospital. He seemed to have forgotten about me. Apart from my mother, I had no one else to turn to for comfort or support. As my siblings all worked or went to school, I had no other family or friends to assist me at the time. While I endured months of agony carrying my first child, doctors were worried because I was getting more and more tired; my stomach continued to swell but the baby refused to drop.

Towards the end of my pregnancy, visits to the hospital were now more frequent and the long journey was excruciating as we had to wake even earlier to get to the hospital due to my size which slowed us down considerably.

When the baby did not appear by the due date, the doctor insisted on inducing labour and I spent more than seventeen hours in pain. Adding insult to injury, my torn vagina was stitched together incorrectly by student doctors and the cut had to be re-stitched, which led to additional time spent in pain and extreme discomfort in the hospital. I was told that I should wash in the bathroom after I got stitched, so I dragged my aching body to the bathroom, where I passed out on the bathroom floor and was discovered by two new shift nurses. I must have been lying there for at least two hours. Women often say that giving birth is the worst type of pain, and my birth experience was a living hell!

I was informed the following day that my new-born baby was severely jaundiced and needed to stay under the ultraviolet light for several days in the intensive care unit. I was released to go home, but my baby remained in the hospital, so I had to make the long trip to the hospital every day to feed and look after the baby before expressing breast milk for his nightly feed. In the public taxi, a few rowdy guys shouted, Girl, you look like a cow," as my breasts had swelled with milk and it was dripping down my shirt. Embarrassed, I endured the stares of fellow passengers.

It was a relief to finally be able to take my baby home to my parents' house in Mitchells Plain, where I slept on the couch cushions, which had now become my bed. Rudi's parents visited for the first time ten days after I gave birth to Solly. The morning of that incident, I was still sleeping with my baby when I heard a loud bang from the front door. When my mother opened the door, Rudi's parents were on the step. I quickly removed the cushions and blankets from the couch and cleaned the living room. They held my baby and ordered me to pack my clothes, saying that I must return to live with them so they could help rear their grandson. Once again, I found myself packed up and carted away like a piece of luggage. It seemed I had no say in the matter, as the adults decided what was best for me and my son, and I was in no position to argue.

When Rudi was introduced to his son for the first time, he showed absolutely zero excitement or enthusiasm, and he certainly wasn't happy to see us or keen to form any bond with his son. He merely went through the motions to please his parents. Rudi continued to study at university with me looking after my baby, but I soon realised that, if I wanted to create a better life for my son and me, I would have to do it for myself, as my husband was still a boy hanging onto his parents' every command.

The clothes his mother bought for me were unfashionable, with long robes and scarves making me look like a dowdy middle-aged woman. I wore the clothes under sufferance as I so badly wanted her approval.

Little Solly was growing up into a beautiful, confident boy. He was already out of his nappies but I was still breastfeeding him. Rudi showed no interest in me or my son and my self-esteem and confidence were at an all-time low.

MECCA

MY IN-LAWS WERE PLANNING A trip to Mecca, and they suddenly got the idea of taking my two-year-old son along with them. My baby was still drinking from my breasts and I was opposed to it. Rudi and his parents put so much pressure on me that I was forced to send my son with them. I cried every day until I was reunited with my son, but he was nothing like the confident, happy and bright toddler I had said goodbye to two months earlier. He reminded me of the cloth dolls I used to make as a child, lifeless and disorientated with panic-stricken eyes. He clung to me when the strange man who brought him back from Mecca handed him to me at the airport.

The child who'd left speaking fluently came back speechless. He was back in nappies and he cried incessantly for his grandmother and after that he wouldn't leave my side, even going to the toilet with me. He peed in the bed till he was twelve years old and never fully recovered his speech.

I only learned much later from an aunt of Rudi what had happened to my son. Rudi's father was sleeping in Mecca and my little Solly had disturbed him. In his anger, he had picked up the child and thrown him against the wall. I was furious; I wanted to kill that man. I blamed myself for my timidity and cowardice in being bullied into allowing them to take my baby. I continued to beat myself up and the guilt consumed me for many years. I became extremely protective over Solly and this continued deep into his adulthood.

Insight:
It was one of my greatest regrets in life that I sent my baby with them. To earn the approval and acceptance of others, I sold out on my baby and myself. In time, I recognised the gift this traumatic event had offered me and was able to forgive myself.

It's only with hindsight that I now see how this incident was a blessing instead of a curse in Solly's life!

As a result of his disability, he worked harder and achieved great success in adulthood instead of taking things for granted. His listening skills became one of his greatest strengths.

THE AFFAIR

RUDI DECIDED TO QUIT VARSITY without finishing his degree to work full-time in his parents' trucking business, which is where his affair started with a girl called Riaana, a slim fair girl who worked with him. During the lunch break, he would blatantly accompany her home so they could spend some time together. Their families became good friends, and it seemed that they accepted that Rudi and Riaana were now a couple. When Rudi's parents returned from a trip to Mecca, it was Riaana who had the honour of choosing several gifts presented to her by my mother-in-law, including expensive jewellery and clothing, while I was given two brass armbands.

One night during the Fast, the two families were having dinner together and in my presence he told everyone at the table that "she" - referring to me – "must go, as I no longer love or want her". I endured sympathetic looks from some of Riaana's aunts and triumphant looks from their parents. They were overjoyed.

"Please don't throw me out. Why don't you love me anymore?" I pathetically begged him in the car while driving home. I was distraught. I felt like I was being thrown away like a dirty rag, but all I got was a look of disgust and repulsion.

My life was looking bleak and dark, so I entered the bathroom and cut my wrist as a cry for help. I had nothing - no education, no money, and no income. I couldn't go back to my parents' house as there was no space. I felt lost.

Rudi found me in the bathroom and took me to our family doctor, who bandaged my wrist, but Rudi was not sympathetic towards me at all. In fact, he was repelled by my actions. He decided to send me and my small son to visit my sister Pat, who had since emigrated to Australia.

I had hit rock bottom in terms of self-esteem. It was a dark space of hopelessness and self-pity for me. My life seemed without purpose. However, I was happy to be given the opportunity to visit Australia, which sounded like my idea of paradise with plenty of sunshine, beautiful beaches, and no apartheid.

AUSTRALIAN TRIP

THE FLIGHT TO AUSTRALIA SEEMED never-ending, especially with a three-year-old boy, but Solly was a very withdrawn and insecure child then, and I had no problem keeping him in his seat and under control. I felt like a zombie on the plane, unsure of where life was taking me. I had no direction and was lost in pain and sadness, a sadness that never fully left my eyes. Even when I smiled or laughed, it hung over me like a cloak. People often commented on how sad I looked, but to me it felt comfortable, as that was all I knew how to be.

I was nervous when we landed at Melbourne Airport but excited to see my sister and her family. The arrival hall was spacious and contained many top-branded shops, in contrast to the two-roomed building that used to house the Cape Town International Airport (before it was renovated).

I was relieved to see my family waiting for us and waving when we finally exited customs; for the first time in my life, I was excited about my holiday and eager to spend time and get to know my nieces and nephew better. They all seemed so happy and healthy. They'd been just little when I'd said goodbye to them ten years earlier.

Life in Australia was very different from life in Cape Town. For the first two weeks, I was severely jetlagged due to the nine-hour time difference between Melbourne and Cape Town, but I eventually became accustomed to the lifestyle and enjoyed the routine. Solly and I would watch some TV as I tried to regain some order in my life after we settled into the household with the kids in school and the adults working.

Pat came home from work one night and announced that she was taking me away for the weekend to New South Wales and that Solly should stay at home with her husband Peter and their children. I was hesitant to leave my baby boy again, but he seemed fine and got on well with the two younger girls. Despite my apprehension, Pat said it would be a delight for me. After all, it was a girls' outing.

I had no idea where we were going when we were all packed and waving goodbye to leave for our weekend away, but I was quite happy to be spending time with my older sister. I saw two men waiting in the lobby of the small casino hotel when we eventually arrived and as we got out of the car one came over and kissed and hugged my sister very passionately. He spoke with a strong Italian accent. The other came over and was introduced to me as the friend of the man who turned out to be my sister's lover.

As they were both much older than I was, and I trusted my sister to protect me, I had no hesitation in being friends with them. After we entered the casino, my sister left with her lover while I remained with this strange older man. He asked if I wanted to play some slots and then he went to change some money into tokens. Since I always ate with my sister's family and did not go out on my own, I did not need money, so I felt somewhat awkward about spending this man's money and then losing it on the machines. We had a lot of fun, and he seemed nice, like an uncle, so I assumed that was how he perceived me. I was only twenty-one years old at the time, very gullible, naive and vulnerable.

Then my sister and her lover returned to the hotel, and we went to reception to get our keys. I was expecting to share a room with my sister, but she took me into a room and the uncle followed her. She left and locked the door from the outside.

I suddenly understood what was happening and panicked as this man started touching me inappropriately. In the beginning, I tried to reason with him by telling him about my situation with my husband, but he was uninterested. While I begged him to leave me alone, he became more irritated with me and accused me of leading him on in the casino, and reminded me of how much money he had spent on me. When he ripped my clothes off and sexually assaulted me, I felt that once again I was the one to blame, unable to move as sobs escaped my throat. I felt numb, empty and cold.

I must have fallen asleep because my sister woke me, warning me not to mention a word to her husband or anyone else. I kept quiet but became visibly withdrawn and went into a deep depression. Since I blamed myself, thinking I had caused the rape, I was too ashamed to tell anyone.

Although I buried this incident along with so many other traumas and pain deep within my psyche, it affected me deeply on so many levels, and I viewed sex as "dirty".

When I returned to Melbourne, there was no more magic or excitement for me, and I couldn't look her husband in the eye as guilt and shame consumed me. The experience had been painful. It felt like I had betrayed him and his trust, and he was a loving, caring individual who didn't deserve that from me. When Rudi finally called me three months later to ask me to come home, after his affair with Riaana ended, I was relieved.

In Cape Town, life continued as usual and I took up various self-improvement courses, such as Dale Carnegie and then a Finishing and Etiquette course, which landed me a modelling job with a local agency. I continued to study subjects such as typing, shorthand, accounting and marketing and became a temp for Nampak and Barpak, and earned a living, which gave me a sense of freedom as I was no longer dependent on Rudi or his parents.

Several months later, I returned from work to Rudi's angry face. He accused me of having an affair in Australia and causing problems in my sister's marriage. My sister's husband Peter had phoned Rudi and told him how I had led her astray. I was dumbfounded by Pat's deception and lost for words when defending myself. As a result, I only spoke to Pat again after she returned to South Africa with her family about ten years later.

Insight:
Although I physically left an abusive relationship, it did not mean that I had transcended that state, but that I was only exchanging one form of abuse for another, as my spiritual state was that of self-hatred, which led to self-abuse. When I abuse myself, I invite others to abuse me. That's how energy vibration operates, attracting our frequency of vibration!

SECOND PREGNANCY

DESPITE OUR DIFFERENCES, RUDI AND I established a good rhythm and decided to make the marriage work as we moved into a three-bedroom house owned by the family trust, and we decided to have another baby since Solly had just turned five and was starting school the following year.

To conceive my second child, I visited a famous fertility specialist, Dr. Sandler, who prescribed fertility drugs that I eventually stopped taking after six months.

One day, my mother called me to tell me that she had heard there was a woman in Mitchells Plain known as Sister Jackie who prayed for people with problems.

Since I had no other immediate options, I decided to try it and went with my mother to a newly built neighbourhood in Mitchells Plain where "Sister Jackie" lived. I was cynical and suspicious of these self-anointed faith healers and sangomas, but I was open to prayer.

The door to the tiny house was opened by the friendly, smiling face of Sister Jackie, who led us through the lounge into a dark bedroom where a candle was lit. "Lie down on the bed and relax," she instructed in a gentle voice. She lifted my dress and rubbed warm olive oil on my abdomen, praying and speaking in tongues. A month later, I discovered I was pregnant! I couldn't believe it, but this whole experience prompted me to be more open-minded about alternatives. I concluded, as a result of my experience, to no longer take these spiritual remedies lightly.

We had been married by Muslim rights. As our marriage was not considered legal in South Africa, and we were expecting our second child, his parents advised us to get married legally to give our children a legal surname. We got married in court and, at the insistence of his parents, we entered into an antenuptial contract. It meant that I had no claim on any of their money or his inheritance.

Rudi seemed repelled by pregnant women, for three months after I feel pregnant he again physically abused me, throwing me against the wall. I immediately felt blood trickling down my leg. I was rushed to the hospital, and my doctor instructed me to lie in the air with my legs up until my foetus had stabilised and it was safe for me to carry my child to full term.

Once again, I had to spend my entire pregnancy living with my parents while my husband moved back to our old home where he was living with his new mistress, Jolene. Jolene had taken over my entire wardrobe. She wore my clothes, slept in my bed, used my perfumes, and had replaced me in Rudi's life.

During my pregnancy, the only thing I looked forward to at the end of the day was my two younger sisters coming home from work with a can of Litchi Esprit. My days were spent helping my mother clean and knitting my baby's clothes, which I was proud to display. However, I did not have money to purchase the necessary nappies, vests and other items needed for my new baby.

My older sister Felicia, who lived next door to my parents with her family, wasn't working, and her husband had an old car that was permanently parked in the driveway because it had a loose gear lever. Someone had to hold the gear lever in place while the driver changed gears and in these desperate times we would hire Leeroy, the neighbour's son, to lie on the floor in the passenger seat, firmly holding the lever in the socket as I drove the car, my big stomach pressed against the steering wheel.

When I was seven months pregnant, I called Rudi to ask for help with baby clothes. Several hours later, I heard his car pull up alongside our house and him calling me to speak with him outside. Arrogantly, he pulled out his chequebook and wrote a check for R3 000. With a smirking gesture, he got back into his car and drove off without greeting me or my family. The following day, I hired Leeroy to hold the gear lever so that I could drive to the bank to cash my cheque, but the teller said there were no funds in the account. I was livid! He intentionally played me for a fool, and I was furious.

"I AM" COURSE

BLOOD BOILING, I HEADED DIRECTLY for the house in Lotus River where he lived with Jolene. His mistress told me that he was taking a course called "I Am" in Green Point. I went into his bedroom because I knew he had a gun under his mattress. As soon as I put it in my bag, I went to Green Point, where the course was being held. I was filled with blind rage. I'd had enough of being mistreated and taken advantage of. I was in a very vulnerable and dark place. Somebody was going to pay. While I had never shot a gun before, I'd watched Rudi shoot targets at the range, and it seemed relatively simple to handle; at least, that's what I thought. My rage was overwhelming, and I wasn't thinking rationally. I had only one goal in mind and that was to kill him.

Pregnant with my second child, and once again forced to walk this path alone, I was consumed by anger and self-pity. When I arrived at the I Am course centre, I demanded to see my husband. I was determined to shoot him. However, they refused to let me see him and it took four men to carry me out and place me on my back on the pavement. Defeated, I returned to Mitchells Plain to await the birth of my second son, as this time I knew the sex of the baby. A week before the baby was due, Rudi came to fetch me and Solly because he had broken up with Jolene and she had left, taking all of my clothes and belongings with her.

Rudi was present at Harry's birth and claimed him as his own. I returned to our home in Lotus River with two small children, breastfeeding one and protecting the other from bullies at the local school, where he suffered constant bullying due to his stutter. We finally decided to move Solly to another school and the only one we found which suited his personality was the Waldorf School in Constantia. The Waldorf teachers work to nurture and engage each child through a curriculum and methodology that integrates academics, arts and practical skills. It is a softer approach to learning and Solly fitted right into the Waldorf community. We couldn't be happier that we chose the right school for my timid and vulnerable child.

In the meantime, my eldest brother Bradley, who'd married a Botswana woman and had moved there, came to live with us temporarily so that he could receive treatment for pancreatic cancer at the hospital. Pancreatic cancer is a particularly deadly form of cancer and he died a few months later, at my parents' house in Mitchells Plain. I was at his side before he passed on and his last words to me were, "Why me?" He made me think about that for a long while.

Insight:
I pondered his death for a long time and only now do I understand that when the Soul no longer grows in this lifetime it chooses to leave the body. It will incarnate in another lifetime to continue the lessons/journey towards Enlightenment.

Rudi raved about the I Am self-improvement course, and after much nagging and persuasion I finally signed up. I was hesitant and very embarrassed to go back to the place where I had made such a fool of myself just a few months earlier, but I did and that course was the catalyst that changed my life so dramatically. Not even in my wildest dreams could I have imagined what was waiting for me!

On the course, I became friends with Aunty Kay, Rudi's father's cousin and mistress. She was a powerful and successful woman who made a lot of money selling curtain remnants and making bedding. I was fascinated by how she carried wads of cash around in her bra and spent huge amounts on a whim. She inspired me with her strength and confidence.

As a child, I had been fascinated by fabrics and their different textures, colour and designs, and I found her fabric business fascinating. The I Am course awakened a deep inner strength I was unaware existed within me, or that I had suppressed. As a result of the short I Am course and Aunty Kay as an example, I felt invincible, like I could conquer the world. With a burning desire to succeed, I set out to do just that!

SUCCESS IS THE BEST REVENGE

ALL THE PENT-UP ANGER I had accumulated - against white people, Indian shopkeepers, my grandmother and family, in-laws, and anyone who made me feel worthless - suddenly took on a life of its own. As a result, I became unstoppable and no obstacle could stop my hunger for success. I was fearless!

I lived by the motto that "Success is the Best revenge"!

Harry was about nine months old in 1985, when I started the Retreat Curtain business.

We had no capital of our own and were given a generous loan of R3 000 by my mother-in-law, which we used to purchase a parcel of second-grade fabric from Svenmill, a fabric manufacturer in the northern suburbs of Cape Town. Additionally, she signed a personal surety for us to open an account with Nettex, a company that manufactures and imports curtain materials, from which we purchased R15 000 worth of goods. With that, we established a household textile factory shop named Retreat Curtain Centre, in a 500m² factory that Rudi's parents owned in 10th Avenue, Retreat, in the industrial area within the coloured residential area. In the beginning, they were generous enough to charge us a very low rent until we were able to pay the normal rent.

Since I had no formal business education, I relied on Rudi and his father to guide me through the legalities of setting up a company. Having accompanied Rudi on multiple occasions when he delivered appliances to their associates, I had seen first-hand how they operated. In addition, I attended auctions, which taught me how to negotiate. Having a good "contact" in business was essential and profitable, and they had to be well "looked after". That was an unwritten business clause that I became familiar with and accepted as the way to conduct business. Furthermore, I learned that what you give out, you generally receive in return.

After we had covered the walls of the factory with some of our fabrics and laid out the few rolls of stock on the long tables, we had only covered a small part of the centre of the factory, with the remnant heap filling one corner.

Rudi and his father decided to sell basic food items such as cooking oil, sugar and some broken crockery bought at auctions to attract locals to the shop. After the initial excitement of the business opening, when locals purchased a few remnants and a few pieces of lay-bye curtaining, turnover and footfall dropped dramatically, and I knew I had to get out of my comfort zone to succeed.

My limited stock of curtaining attracted a few of the locals but I realised that, unless I diversified my merchandise, I was not going to make a success of my business, so I decided to venture into new markets and bought a consignment of towels. I decided to sell my new stock on Mitchells Plain station. As I did not have a car, I had to drag the box of towels onto the train and down the steps to reach the crowds, where I stood all day in the sun. Even though things were tough, I didn't allow myself to become demotivated or embarrassed. I had one single goal and that was to succeed at all costs!

Rudi and his father eventually left the shop to open a hardware store in Athlone Industria. As I needed to increase sales, I printed black and white pamphlets to drop around the neighbourhood. As a result of this, I needed Harry's nanny Angelina to watch over him and the shop in my absence.

As a consequence of my marketing, more and more people started to pop in. I bought Angelina an industrial sewing machine and taught her how to sew tablecloths and other household items from the remnants.

Harry's playground became the remnant pile and Solly would play on the heap with his little brother after school, where he would collect small remnants that he carried home with him and that eventually grew into a big pile in the corner of his bedroom.

Christmas orders for table doily sets started coming in from our local customers. Then we copied a bedspread we purchased from a supplier and that became a big hit. We sewed bedspreads between tending to Harry and helping the odd customer who ventured into the shop, but now most of our sales came from frilled bedspreads and pillowcases sold through agents at factories in our area.

I built up a strong customer base for ready-made sets, which consisted of a polyester floral bedspread with matching curtains. I started recruiting agents from nearby factories who sold this on a six-month credit basis, and they would either bring the money they collected on a Saturday, or I would go to their houses to collect.

Due to the growth of this type of business, I needed another person with an administrative background to manage this division of the business, since I was more involved in growing the custom fabric division. That was when I hired Mrs. Louw, who was just the right person for the job. She was a very stern, "no nonsense" kind of woman and even I felt intimidated by her.

Later, I was able to secure a stall at the Grand Parade in the city. This boosted the business and opened another avenue for a different type of merchandise which was the lace curtain business. The majority of my customers came from the African townships as well as foreign African buyers who, after a while, started buying in bulk from me. I became known for my wholesale lace curtaining and supplied smaller market stallholders throughout Cape Town with the merchandise.

Over time, we branched out into small upcountry towns such as Calvinia, Caledon and Ceres and employed agents in the area. Once we'd collected orders, we packed the van and drove out to these towns on a Saturday afternoon or Sunday to deliver the orders to the agents. My merchandise was still only appealing to the coloured community, and I had no idea how to attract the more affluent customer.

To learn how to calculate fabric quantities for windows, I pretended to be a customer at exclusive curtain boutiques and requested fictitious quotations. At that time our company was only selling wide-width polyester fabric, which was easy to figure out. We only doubled the amount of fabric by the size of the window.

Even though Angelina Louw and Mrs. Louw sometimes made curtains for customers in their spare time, most of them sewed their own curtains.

My first break came when I discovered a company called Fabric Library. After I bought a parcel of second-grade fabrics from them at R2 per metre, I could afford to buy an ad in the Cape Town Argus where I advertised this fabric for R2.99 per metre and it was a hit! There were customers from all over Cape Town who queued up outside the Retreat Factory, and I was unable to meet the demand. Tommy, the newspaper representative, became one of my most trusted friends and his support enabled me to become Cape Town's leading curtain retailer through the Argus ads.

My merchandise changed from mainly polyester to include cotton prints, Taichung, linen, and other combinations of synthetic and natural fabrics. As a consequence, my knowledge increased accordingly. Since I was now serving a new customer base which demanded a different service, I had to learn more about interior decor and design and colour combinations.

I had to learn very quickly about the various types of fabrics. as I embarrassed myself quite a few times by not knowing what I was selling and being caught out by a more knowledgeable customer. My customer base grew as my name got around and I was attracting more affluent clients from as far away as Camps Bay, Somerset West and Stellenbosch. I had finally broken through the barrier, and we were now attracting a different type of customer who demanded make-up and sizing services.

After establishing a new department and learning new lessons, the company entered the custom curtain and upholstery make-up business. Through trial and error, we were able to develop the department into a successful business, with more than twenty employees.

CURTAIN QUEEN

THE ARRIVAL OF THE FASHIONABLE duvet in South Africa instead of sheets and blankets led to an explosion in demand for duvet covers. I visited Berg River Textiles in Paarl, where I met Mr. Ramsay, the sales manager. I had struck gold!

I was given an exclusive contract to sell their 230cm-wide second-grade sheeting to the public, as well as home business owners. When the Berg River truck delivered new stock every week, there were queues of customers, and I couldn't keep up with the demand. With this kind of merchandise in my shop, I became the shop of choice for the home sewing industry.

After getting my foot into the government circle, I won some bids for curtains for local government buildings.

During my marketing campaign, I offered handsome commissions to estate agents and architectural offices in exchange for customer referrals. We landed hotel contracts, and the Retreat Curtain Centre became a respected and reputable business.

Within one year I opened my second shop in Athlone, a 3rd in Maitland, where after I bought my first commercial building in Claremont and opened a boutique decor shop called Curtain Queen.

With my visible success, I became the darling of the curtain industry in Cape Town, with every company rep my friend, all offering me their redundant and seconds stock that I promptly sold out. By 1994, I had enough stock to fill ten shops. I took on the status of "royalty" in the community and was dubbed "The Curtain Queen".

I began attending company functions, new fabric launches, and dining in fancy restaurants with my various suppliers. I was initially intimidated by this, as I had never been exposed to restaurant etiquette before. I had only ever used a fork as cutlery. Therefore, I was uncomfortable and confused about table manners, and I embarrassed myself many times by using the wrong piece of cutlery from the plethora of knives and forks on the table. My companions politely pretended they did not see my hesitation and discomfort. Consequently, I enrolled in an etiquette school that gave me the knowledge and poise to attend these functions with confidence.

My vision was to purchase my own buildings and trade from there and my first model of the Curtain Queen shop proved successful. With my visible success, I managed to secure finance for a shop in Kuils River, Somerset West, Montague Gardens, and Paarden Eiland. I purchased a 3 000 square metre building on Lily Road in Retreat, which became my main store and head office.

Intending to franchise some of my branches, I renamed my organisation Curtain Warehouse to encompass all the areas in Cape Town and thus expanded my business.

With Curtain Warehouse's explosion on the market, a whole new world had opened up for me. I became the preferred supplier of curtain and upholstery fabrics. I was offered flights and five-star hotel accommodation around South Africa by companies who wanted to get rid of their surplus stock.

Customers, including corporations, hotels and government agencies, flooded in. I was frequently featured in the local media. We had a thriving business, and employed more than 100 employees at our various shops.

At the same time, I formed a residential rental property company and purchased dilapidated houses and apartments in good areas such as the Atlantic Seaboard and southern suburbs, which I refurbished with the help of Rudi. With so many tenants I had to employ a maintenance team as well as a separate rent collection office.

My passion and dreams, coupled with suppressed anger, created an unstoppable force of energy that saw no obstacles, but only opportunities, and with this force of energy came material wealth. There was "no mountain too high to climb, nor a sea too deep to swim in", for it was all part of the journey.

RUDI BUSINESS CRASH

RUDI'S HARDWARE BUSINESS BOOMED AND then crashed during this period. Rudi and his "Mr. Nice Guy" approach led him to trust his staff with confidential information; a mistake that led to his downfall.

He suffered from a deep depression and he became a stay-at-home dad, which gave me peace of mind knowing he was taking care of the children.

In his need for self-validation, he humiliated me constantly by touching and making sexual advances towards my unmarried sisters and friends, making them feel uncomfortable. Rather than being blatantly rude to him, they complained to me. He singled out my sister Cat, who sometimes lived with us, and even asked her to be his "second wife".

My parents and family had also moved to Zeekoevlei and my mother and all my sisters were working for me, managing the branches spread all over the Cape. I was proud that I was able to give them something back after growing up with them in such modest surroundings. Finally, my mother was extremely proud of me and took her job very seriously, watching over everything like a hawk!

Despite my change in fortunes, I never truly claimed my success. I was extremely modest and attributed my success to

Rudi. It felt like I wasn't the one who made it, and if I had owned it I would have felt like a fraud. Though I had no money problems, managing my staff, travelling extensively, and taking care of my children became too much for me

RELIGION

I DECIDED TO CONVERT BACK to Christianity when I realised I could no longer live my life as a Muslim, for I was simply trying to please my in-laws. As a result, my father-in-law was incensed. He was so angry that he invited us over for dinner one night and asked me to go into his bedroom. He requested that I listen to an audio recording, locked the door behind him, and left me there before joining his wife and son in the kitchen. The recording was filled with obscenities and insults directed at me and the Christian faith.

In the recording, I was accused of being lower than a pig and told that the sea could never erase the sin from my soul as a Christian. As the recording ended, the door was unlocked and the three of them stood outside, sneering at me. With tears streaming down my cheeks, I walked straight to the front door and left. My husband's complicity in this vicious plot left me feeling deeply betrayed.

The incident served to re-ignite the feeling of not being good enough, which later manifested itself in many ways throughout my life, as I vowed to become even more successful than I was already! While I didn't have a clear idea of what "even more successful" meant, I simply knew in my heart that the sky was the limit.

ZEEKOEVLEI

WITHIN ONE YEAR I HAD built such a strong business that I was able to buy my first house, a double-story in Zeekoevlei, an area I'd always wanted to live in. Zeekoevlei borders a huge freshwater lake on the Cape Flats and the name means "hippopotamus marsh". It has amazing views of Table Mountain, but it was classified as a "white area", so I was forbidden to buy the house in my name and had to form a company with my white lawyer who stood as my nominee and became a trusted friend.

When I moved into my home, I was overjoyed to see the lake from the upper floor, but unfortunately my home wasn't near the water's edge.

A couple of years later, I sold my first house because it wasn't on the water's edge. I then bought a 2000-metre plot on the water's edge in Zeekoevlei, which was right up Rudi's alley. He constructed the ultimate house, by hiring top artisans, since money was not an issue, including a huge swimming pool and a tennis court surrounded by professionally designed landscaping.

I bought a speed boat and entertained on a grand scale, so I was never short of friends stopping by to enjoy both the relaxed atmosphere and the lake's beauty. As a VIP at many restaurants, I regularly took over entire establishments for birthday parties and celebrations with my family and friends.

Taliep Petersen sang at one of my parties at the Southern Sun. For various reasons, I loaned money to friends and family, never to get it back. Each year, I took my children on extended winter holidays to different countries, where we stayed in five-star hotels.

The business was booming and growing and life was good! Perhaps too good?

FAMILY LIFE

SOLLY AND HARRY BOTH ATTENDED the Waldorf school and enjoyed living amongst their friends who lived nearby. Solly became quite popular and had many friends, mainly boys, visiting him at home. He was a confused teenager, always searching and aspiring to be someone other than who he was. At one stage he became Jewish, then he grew his hair like a Rastafarian, but he would not choose Christianity or Islam for fear of offending one of his parents. Solly was a creative boy and did not like to take part in any type of sport.

Harry, on the other hand, was a quiet and confident boy who excelled at sports. At one point, he played for Western Province and had the ability to move on to the next level, but he didn't quite believe he could achieve it. He has a brilliant scientific mind and mathematics is one of his favourite subjects, yet he is an amazing artist as well, a rare combination indeed.

Harry took part in many theatre plays and was confident and eloquent on stage. He had all the attributes for a successful and great future.

After his father moved out, Harry took on the role of protector of his family. Harry has a personality of one who is extremely loyal and will fight for those he loves.

Rudi was never close to Solly, and abused him verbally, emotionally and physically whenever he could, taking out his frustrations on the poor boy. Solly remained a very anxious and withdrawn child. The only thing he wanted was his father's attention and approval, so he was always very nervous when his father was around. Many times, Rudi would beat and kick Solly to a pulp. I felt helpless to assist and he justified this abuse as discipline. On one occasion, his father lost his temper and threw a knife at him, which pierced his stomach. Often, my son and I would run to my parents' house to escape Rudi's wrath. In many instances, I took the punches aimed at Solly. He was jealous of Solly and accused me of loving my son more than I loved him. Of course I loved my son more, as he was timid and vulnerable and I was all he had.

My two boys got on well and would often support each other when their father abused one or both of them. I often heard them repeat the Childline number: 0800123231 toll-free.

Speech and drama classes are an important part of the Waldorf curriculum. Solly participated in the annual classroom play during his early primary school years, but it was mostly in groups or background parts where he was not expected to speak much. One year, however, he was given the lead role in a play. I eagerly awaited his appearance as Rudi and I sat in one of the front rows of the theatre. When he entered the stage, he froze and could not say anything. Everyone in the room was sympathetic when he stammered so badly, but Rudi, ashamed and embarrassed for his son, got up and left. Solly remained on stage as one of the more confident boys spoke on his behalf.

Tears rolled down my face as I watched my son struggle to speak, and I was immensely proud of his courage and determination to stay until the end of the play.

THE BUBBLE HAD TO BURST

MY SHOP WAS LOCATED IN a coloured industrial area that had a high crime rate. I witnessed a murder in front of my shop one Saturday morning. As I approached my shop, I had to stop due to two men fighting in the middle of the road. One of the men broke a bottle and the other one was stabbed in the neck with the head of the broken bottle. I watched in horror as blood spurted from his neck and within a few minutes he was dead. I watched as the murderer calmly walked away. It was horrific to see someone kill another and not even run away from the scene. Instead, he walked away as if nothing had happened.

As a result of this incident, I came to realise how little my life meant to others but how valuable my life is to me. I was reminded about my purpose in this lifetime, but I was not ready to embrace it.

One Friday night, we were awoken by the security company telling us that Retreat's main shop had been broken into. A closer inspection revealed that the burglars had accessed the shop through the broken window. Because the shop was packed to capacity, I couldn't put a value on the stolen items. There were many rolls of fabric, duvet covers and lace curtains that had been stolen.

We had just received ninety-five huge boxes of imported lace curtaining that had yet to be unpacked and I was concerned a repeat would occur. Rudi agreed to fix the window before the next weekend. Despite his promises all week, the window was still broken by Friday afternoon. A very unsavoury man entered the shop looking suspicious, as if checking out the security and alarm system. Rudi was relaxing at home when I called him and begged him to come up and fix the window, explaining my fears and suspicions. He assured me that nothing would happen and that the burglars wouldn't be audacious enough to return, but my fears were realised when the burglars returned and stole all of the boxes of expensive lace that had been delivered the previous day.

I was shattered! This was the final straw! Rudi's laziness and failure to accept responsibility for his life had become too much of a liability to me and it was time to cut ties. That Monday morning, I went to a divorce lawyer without telling Rudi. He got the wake-up call when the sheriff served the divorce papers a few weeks later and he immediately moved out.

A few months later, the divorce was final, and I became a single mom with more responsibilities than I could handle. My children were devastated, and I was unable to comfort them or support them adequately because I was also going through the pain of losing my marriage. I was managing five large shops with approximately eighty employees who depended on me. He was stupefied by the divorce as he never thought I would do what I had threatened. At least he continued to visit the house and lift the kids to and from school, which helped a lot.

Rudi and some Waldorf parents planned to take their children rafting down the Orange River during the school holidays. I invited my nephew Pierre, Jeff's son, because one of the boys cancelled, so there was space for one more child. I thought he might enjoy it as he had never been on this type of camping trip before.

He was excited and probably a bit apprehensive as he was a very shy and withdrawn young man, but he was close to Harry who was only six years old. All of them set off in the company van but returned the following day when Pierre went missing while swimming across the river with Harry. Both sides of the river had been combed in hopes that he might have gotten lost. Finally, they decided to end the search and returned home without him. Both Harry and Solly were traumatised as Harry described how Pierre went down under the water while they were swimming side by side.

Rudi did not come to the house to explain the situation but went straight to the flat at his parents' house, where he locked himself up, refusing to open the door to Pierre's parents, who were begging for information about their missing son. Eventually, Solly led Jeff and his wife Lynn back to the Orange River where they searched for Pierre's body with help from the local lifeguards. They found him exactly where he had disappeared, based on Harry's description.

It was a difficult time for my family and my children were traumatised and I sought out therapy for both of them. Their world had been shattered by the death of their cousin, and I was unable to provide support to them.

I was disgusted and angry at the cowardly way Rudi handled Pierre's parents and, at the same time, I was riddled with guilt for being the one who'd invited him on this fatal trip.

Insight:

As humans, we are unable to understand why a child or young person dies, but in truth the Soul came to earth to learn or complete a lesson from a previous life and, when it's complete, it'll depart from this life, leaving a lasting memory for the human race of how precious life is, and that Love is the only truth!

Pierre was truly an angel who came to shed light and love on his short stay on earth.

ITALIAN FABRICS

IN SOUTH AFRICA, I DID not completely feel at home. In addition, I felt inferior and resentful towards white South Africans, especially those who spoke Afrikaans, as it reminded me of my "coloured" identity, which translated as "less than". Due to the limitations I had as a coloured woman in SA, I felt insecure about expanding my business beyond Cape Town. However, when I travelled overseas, I felt like a different person - confident, beautiful and admired. Therefore, when the opportunity to do business in Europe came up, I grabbed it with both hands. I was now ready to take my curtain business to the next level, which meant selling international brands exclusively through my outlets.

I was attracting more discerning clients. A large percentage of them were from Europe and spent their winter in their mansions in Constantia and the Atlantic seaboard. We referred to them as "swallows", as these birds migrate to warmer climates during winter. I envied their lifestyle; I can't handle the cold weather. When the weather is dark and grey, I get downright miserable. I adore and worship the sun. It makes me happy and joyful. It reminds me of butterflies and birds singing in my garden, those are times when I become a child again. I silently promised that I too would become a "swallow" one day.

These discerning customers demanded quality, class and more exclusive and exotic fabrics. Cottons and linens were some of the natural fabrics that were in high demand.

Having heard of Heimtexil, the largest textile fair held in Frankfurt, Germany, at the beginning of the year, I decided to make that my next destination. The fair was overwhelming, with more than a thousand stalls filled with beautifully decorated fabrics, many of which were sold by experienced personnel in sophisticated marketing side-shows. The huge exhibition floor was divided into European, Asian and Indian quarters and was an intimidating onslaught to the visual senses for rookie little me. I walked around, absorbing the experience of just being there. The "hip" attire of jeans, takkies and a black leather jacket seemed out of place among the tailored, classic outfits that oozed sophistication and wealth. Despite having a healthy bank account, my background of hawking and clawing my way out of poverty made me realise that I had entered a different world of business. The first step was to dress as if I belonged there.

Up until this point, I had felt comfortable bargaining for discounts, buying lots and wheeling and dealing, but this was a new way of doing business and communicating that I had never experienced before. I was intimidated when I was invited to sit down with a glass of French champagne to discuss fabric ranges that required a minimum order of a thousand metres per colour.

AMBROGIO

I BELIEVE IT WAS MY guardian angel that led me to Mr. Ambrogio's stand, a place that screamed quality and design that welcomed both the humble and experienced. Ambrogio was not a handsome man by any stretch of the imagination, but his kind, charismatic warmth enveloped me - the waif from Africa - with genuine inclusion and an understanding of my quaint naivety.

He talked to me as a friend and smiled without being condescending when I pulled out my wads of notes to start bargaining. "Rather keep those hidden and spend some of it on an outfit," he suggested gently, like a wise, knowledgeable father. He pulled out his notepad and wrote an address on it, which is where the taxi took me the following morning. It was a designer clothing market where I purchased three exquisite silk suits with shoes to match. Ambrogio almost fell off his chair when I showed up later that day, telling me that I looked like I'd stepped off the cover of Vogue! Thanks to him, I returned to

South Africa more confident, more sophisticated, and infinitely more knowledgeable about the international trading game.

Ambrogio invited me to visit the Proposte Fair, which takes place every April in a historic villa on Lake Como. I had never heard of Lake Como and upon my return to South Africa, I planned my next buying trip to Como.

The first time I saw Como, I instantly fell in love with the place. Its beauty and perfection were exactly how I had pictured heaven to be. I silently promised myself I would return again and again. I was invited to Ambrogio's factory, where I cleared his shelves of the finest upholstery fabrics - chenilles, Italian silks, satins, linen, velvets, and more, at a fraction of the regular price.

Having this type of merchandise propelled me to the next level and now I was competing against my local suppliers with even better products at a fraction of the price.

I had to learn eco-trading terms since I was now importing almost all of my stock from European manufacturers. After my local sheeting supply dried up, I became a frequent traveller, with trips to Pakistan, India and China, where I bought containers of sheeting.

As my business continued to grow, my responsibilities increased as I juggled raising two children, travelling and managing my ever-expanding business. The money kept rolling in and my standard of living increased to include extended holidays overseas with my kids. Five-star hotels, private planes, luxury cars and holiday houses in False Bay and Sea Point became the norm.

I was obsessed with my pursuit of success, and this drive fuelled me to achieve even greater heights. In addition, I was passionate about creating with colours and fabrics. For me, that was even more exciting than the money.

Insight:
Money has never motivated me. Living my passion was my main motivation. I had used my anger positively by building a successful business.

FAMILY WORKERS

AMIDST MY RAPIDLY GROWING SUCCESS, Pat had since returned from Australia with her family to settle back in Cape Town and was amazed at my huge operation. In Pat's mind, because she'd married a white man, she was superior. When she saw my business and how I lived, she wanted to be part of it.

Considering how we'd parted ten years previously and our chequered history, I decided to bury the hatchet and move on.

It was my pleasure to hire her to manage one of my big stores in Maitland with the help of my sister Felicia. Fran became manageress of my Claremont store and my youngest sister Ava and my sister-in-law, who had also joined the company, ran the big store in Kuils River. As a result of the success I had, I paid my sisters a generous salary to boost and empower them. My desire to please my family led me to overcompensate in many ways, to the detriment of my other staff members, who in retrospect must have felt marginalised and discriminated against.

One day, I received an unexpected call from a staff member of the shop that Pat managed informing me of my sister's dishonesty. She had been driving rolls of fabric away after hours and planned to open her own business. I confronted her and she left my company. Unbeknown to me, with the help of my mother's youngest sister, Mavis, she contracted five guys from Lavender Hill to hurt me in my shop. When I returned from lunch one day, I saw my mother anxiously waiting outside the store, and as soon as she saw me, she ran to the car, yelling, "Libbet, get back into the car and go. Aunt Mavis is inside with five gangsters. They've been waiting for you with knives, so please just get out of here fast," she blurted out. Panicking, I drove off in a rush to get out of there.

Pat opened a fabric shop in Muizenberg, which turned out to be a huge failure. So, after six months she closed it, sold her house, and the family returned to Australia. As she did not quite get her revenge, she made one last attempt to hurt me by telling my mother-in-law that "I slept my way to the top".

I simultaneously discovered the fraud that had been committed at my other branches by Fran at my Claremont shop and Ava at the Kuils River branch. Further investigation by my accountant revealed that large amounts of money and stock had been stolen, which prompted me to take legal action.

BETRAYAL

MY SISTERS WERE ALL IN cahoots, and those who weren't directly involved knew what was going on and chose to stay quiet about it. I was devastated by the betrayal. I'd thought I could trust the people to whom I gave so much. After all, they were my family, and family is supposed to protect and love each other, or so I believed.

My sister Ava, the baby of the family whom we all spoiled, was someone I trusted with my life. I often paid for her overseas holidays and other privileges because I wanted only the best for her. I made her manager of my Kuils River store, which was one of my most prestigious and busiest shops, after her marriage to Randy, an Indian man from Durban.

Angelina, Harry's nanny, had since been transferred to work at my Kuils River shop. She was a hard worker and extremely honest and loyal towards the company. It was Angelina who blew the whistle on Ava's dishonesty and, initially, I did not want to believe Angelina when she told me about her suspicions. After requesting the books from Ava, she concealed them by burying them under a tree outside of the shop, but Angelina saw where she had buried them and brought them to me after work. The discovery blew my mind!

As a result of a thorough audit, my accountant was able to track some of the third-party checks deposited into her account at Standard Bank, where her husband worked as a teller. Besides the undeclared cash sales, which were difficult to calculate, the number of recorded checks and bank transfers which were fraudulently deposited into her personal bank account was staggering.

I was angry and extremely disappointed, and I wanted to hold her accountable, but when I confronted her she went on a rampage to destroy me. She reported me to various government agencies for misconduct and dishonesty and, when that didn't work, her husband bought a gun and threatened to shoot me.

Because of his vicious temper and violent nature, I didn't take his threats lightly because when he got angry he became reckless and fearless.

As a result, I had to leave my home and my kids for a few weeks until things settled down. Three months later, their three-year-old boy drowned in their swimming pool. I loved him as if he was my own.

Ava asked my forgiveness when we were at his hospital bed, which I immediately gave with a big hug. I would have done anything to save her from the severe pain and loss.

I would never have wished this on her or anyone else.

My mother was watching over him while Ava and her husband went to the doctor with their three-week-old daughter. While my mother was watching her favourite soapie, the little boy fell into the pool and they found him floating face down sometime later. He was brain dead and died soon after in hospital.

He drowned exactly six months after Pierre's drowning, and his death shattered the entire family.

Ava went off the rails, and Randy tried to drown his sorrows in alcohol. They started having problems in their marriage and he sought comfort in a female colleague's arms. When Ava found out, she went crazy. She disappeared from the house and he frantically searched all over for her.

Then, one Saturday afternoon, he pulled up at my house demanding that I tell him where Ava was. Ava had a very close lady friend called Saby and he knew they were together. He swore that he was going to hurt Ava and her girlfriend, who he believed was leading her astray. After he almost hit the wall while pulling into my driveway, I saw that he was completely inebriated. I became anxious as soon as he stepped out of the car, holding a half bottle of brandy in one hand and a gun in the other.

I ran into the small cottage on my property, which my friend Gavin was renting from me. Randy, staggering, followed me inside and in a slurring, hostile tone started interrogating me. "Where is Ava?" he asked.

"I have no idea. She is probably with her girlfriend, Saby," I replied.

He suddenly became violently angry, yelling obscenities and demonstrating how he would shoot her friend, Saby. He placed the gun to his forehead and pulled the trigger. I closed my eyes, expecting the worst. I heard it click and sighed when I realised the gun had not gone off.

"Please give me the gun," I pleaded, but he became even more agitated. Once again, he demonstrated by pointing the gun to his forehead and pulling the trigger.

Gavin and I were stunned by the deafening sound the gun produced, as I had assumed it was empty. In horror, we watched as his body crumpled in slow motion, landing in an awkward heap on the cement floor. I did not stay to check whether he was dead or alive. I jumped up and hysterically fled the scene.

We waited for almost an hour for the ambulance to come to pick him up. As he was still lying in the same position, and we were uncertain if he were alive or not, we decided to transport him to the nearest hospital on the back of the company van.

After a long wait, the doctor finally arrived to inform Ava that the bullet was lodged in part of his brain that was too sensitive to be operated on. Because his eyes had been irreversibly damaged, he would be blind for the rest of his life. Sadly, he committed suicide a few years later, after he was diagnosed with cancer, by gassing himself in his car.

I received a letter written by one of my sisters, whom I assumed to be Ava or Pat, accusing me of being a witch and causing the deaths of my two nephews.

LEO

ANGELINA WAS PROMOTED TO BRANCH manager of Kuils River after Ava left. I completely trusted and believed in the abilities of Angelina when it came to managing the branch. On a Friday evening, after 6pm, a man entered the shop and asked Angelina to sell him a lot of our ready-made bedding. When he had finished selecting a variety of bedspreads and duvets, he told Angie he had a cheque for R10 000 to pay for the items.

She accepted the cheque and asked him to wait a few minutes. She quietly put the cheque into the special verification machine and it came up as "stolen". Without alerting the man, Angie called the police, who within minutes arrived and arrested the man, who claimed he had been sent by Leo, who was parked around the corner. The police took the man to Leo's car, where they found him waiting in his car. They arrested him as well. Leo was allowed to make one phone call, which he made to Jeff (my older brother) and told Jeff to warn me to drop the charges since he knew many gangsters from Lavender Hill who he could hire to get me killed. To protect me and my children from some of my vicious, jealous, and dangerous siblings who would stop at nothing to hurt me, I dropped all charges.

I did not lay eyes on him again for many years and when I did somehow bump into him it was as if this incident had never happened.

My siblings were all angry at being found out. They waged a war of sorts. There were no emotional scenes, as my family doesn't deal with emotional issues. No one ever apologised for the betrayal and hurt they had caused me and it was expected of me just to accept and carry on as if this kind of behaviour was normal.

My mother did her best to remain neutral. I had no one to turn to because she was in a difficult position.

This was when God carried me.

All I ever wanted was for them to share in my success and prosper with me, to be proud of me, and above all to approve of me. Never did I imagine that my success would cause them to hate me to the point that they would even want to hurt me and steal from me. While experiencing this betrayal by my siblings, I made a discovery that changed my life forever!

Insight:

After I forgave my siblings for the betrayal, I realised forgiveness is a selfish act since it freed me from the resentment that I was carrying around with me as a way of punishing them, but I realised I was only punishing myself.

For as long as I continued to blame others for my pain and hurt, I didn't have to take responsibility for my part in it. In blaming them, I lost sight of the gift it had brought me. They were the physical manifestation to show me how I betrayed myself over and over, and if I couldn't trust myself, how could I trust someone else?

COLLAPSE

DURING THIS UNSTABLE TIME, MY mother asked Cat and me to accompany her to an uncle's house because he was dying of cancer. Although extremely preoccupied, I made an exception to accommodate her and visited this uncle. We pulled up to a small council house near my shop and knocked on the front door. When the door opened, I froze in disbelief as I stared into a reflection of my face, just on a male's body. I recognised it as my Uncle John's, who I hadn't seen for almost twenty years. Cat and I stared at each other, as shocked expressions registered on our faces!

I felt dizzy, my head spun, and I tried to speak, but no words emerged; it was all there in front of me! As pieces of the puzzle started falling in place, I began remembering my childhood like it was a slow-motion movie. In a split second, my entire foundation had collapsed! The evidence was so obvious I couldn't deny it even if I wanted to. The betrayal by the very people I trusted with my whole being was too much to comprehend.

"Who am I?" I repeated this question to myself over and over as my foundation crumbled into a million pieces. Everything felt surreal. I tried to make sense of it but at that moment nothing made sense. I began questioning everything; simple words like "the" made me wonder about their meanings and why they would mean that. I questioned nature, humanity and life,

My mind was numb, confused and disorientated as I again went into hiding, not ready to face or accept the truth as I already knew it but struggled to accept it. I am the product of an illegitimate and shameful relationship; a bastard!

A few days later, I plucked up the courage to speak with my mother. She was waiting as I had been avoiding her since my discovery!

I will always remember these words she quoted as we sat down to talk. "What we sweep under the carpets, the crows will shout from rooftops," she said.

I understood but I needed to know the story. "How could you have lied to me all this time?" I demanded in an angry tone.

"Libbet," she said, "I was ordered to marry George by my mother but I was not in love with him. He was my sister's boyfriend and like a brother to me. I tried to make it work with him, but then I fell in love with John, who is your father." She went on to say, "You are our love child".

Her words shattered me. I felt dirty and ashamed of where I came from, the product of a sleazy affair. I wanted the truth, but I wasn't ready to hear it!

She begged me for forgiveness, but I couldn't find it in my heart to forgive her, not just yet. I was angry and felt deeply betrayed.

Sobbing, after speaking with her I confronted my father. "You knew all along you were not my father," I said accusingly.

Tears streaming down his cheeks, he lovingly told me, "I am your father, and you will always be my daughter. I love you."

Heart-wrenching sobs burst from my very being, and I fled to bury myself in my misery. I was broken. I no longer had an identity. Everything I had ever known was a lie. I was a lie!

Over time, as I attempted to piece my life back together, I came to realise how kind, strong and loving my father was. As a child, I once thought of my father as weak, a pushover. Now I see what a saint my father was, in his ability to care for another man's child and his love and adoration for my mother despite her betrayal. The gratitude for having him as my father overwhelmed me and once again I realised how special I was!

Several months later, Uncle John passed away, and I went to the funeral with my mother and Cat. As the priest was reading the obituary on the podium, he mentioned that John had left eight children and two illegitimate children who were present at the service. The entire congregation turned to stare at us, some with utter contempt in their eyes. At that moment, I wanted to be swallowed whole by the earth. My head bowed downward as I walked out of the church, ashamed to face the people staring at us as if we were aliens.

During this time, I became ill. I was haemorrhaging blood and unable to focus on my business. I was too traumatised to give any attention to my children. After hearing sobs from Solly's bedroom one night, I went upstairs and found him taking pills in the bathroom as he attempted to commit suicide. I was horrified to witness my son's actions. He was not able to cope with what was happening in our lives. Solly fell into my arms sobbing and I held onto him as I so desperately wanted to save him from the pain. Despite being so broken, we found strength in comforting each other as we sat on the bathroom floor together.

After I'd tucked Solly back into his bed, I slipped into my bed and sobbed until I felt I might suffocate on my tears. I asked God, "Where are You? Why all this pain?" I must have fallen into a strange, fitful sleep because I had a strange out-of-body experience while I was asleep.

I found myself up against the ceiling, gazing down at my body, arms lying limply on both sides with open hands. My face looked skew, as if it were a corpse. Then I experienced being tossed around in a dark vortex and, after what seemed an eternity, was flung out into a brilliant white light which embraced me with so much love that, when I woke up the following morning, I knew I was loved and protected by a higher power who was always watching over me.

Insight:
Only in hindsight, do I understand that Uncle John was an angel who showed me that I was a princess and worthy of love.

I was privileged to have had two fathers who loved and adored me!

SEA CAPTAIN RUNE

AFTER I GOT DIVORCED, I went to the V&A Waterfront with some friends and met a handsome Norwegian with bright blue eyes and blonde hair who was the captain of a cargo ship. We started dating soon after.

We communicated by writing letters to each other, as it was the only way we could keep in touch. Three months after his departure from Cape Town, I received a letter inviting me to visit him and his family for the Christmas holidays. I thoroughly enjoyed spending time with his family and friends in his hometown, Arendal, located in the north-eastern part of Norway.

I was eager to learn to ski in the scenic mountains, but I ended up sliding on my backside down the steep slopes.

At the end of our idyllic holiday, he proposed to me, but I was not ready to take the marriage step again just yet, and instead we got engaged. I was relieved that my kids liked Rune.

Upon hearing that I had a boyfriend, Rudi went crazy and pursued me endlessly once more. It went on for a year, with him threatening Rune and chasing him with a gun at one point. Eventually, Rune gave up on me and left South Africa. I made up with Rudi yet again. However, he did not move back into the house, since he was very happy to visit, then return home where he could do as he pleased. This of course included dating other women while seeing me. Rudi became obsessed with his body and looks and started going to the gym for hours every day.

I only understood later why Rudi became obsessed with the gym. It was because he had met another woman named Zea and they started dating.

Although I occasionally went to Constantia Virgin Active to work out, I was usually too exhausted when I got home after work to do so, and I preferred to be with my children.

Being very busy running both a huge retail chain and managing a property company with many tenants, I was unaware of the affair. My days were packed and I had very little time to wonder what my ex-husband was doing. It wasn't until my friends and regular customers told me he'd been seen in public with her that I realised something serious was happening. When I confronted him, he denied it, but one night I saw them leaving the gym together.

In a fit of blind rage, I confronted him, hysterically attacking him verbally, and vowing to do everything in my power to get even with him. My words were silenced by his fists pounding my face. I was thrown to the ground, bleeding from my mouth and nose as his boots kicked into my stomach and ribs. I was curled up in pain and humiliation when I saw Zea looking down on me with a smirk as they walked over to his car and drove off, leaving me to fend for myself.

I was unable to lift myself off the ground because of my injuries. Ava came to my rescue as I was limping badly. She helped me into the car and drove me directly to the police station to lay a charge of assault. I had to get medical care as my face and body were severely bruised and had to convalesce at home until I could show my face at my business again.

Rudi was summoned to court, where the magistrate happened to be an old school friend of his, and he got off scot-free!

Rudi stayed away for many months after that incident, never even visiting the children. One day, out of nowhere, he reappeared, and life went on as if the affair and abuse had never occurred. I realised that this was the nature of our love-hate relationship. This time, he assured me, the affair was over and that he wanted to be an active father for his children.

Had I forgiven him or was I just burying the pain as I had done my entire life?

Insight:
As humans, we would view this as betrayal and abuse but in soul terms it was the pain and suffering my soul needed to grow and transcend to the next level.

I attracted Rudi into my life as at the time my spiritual state was one of self-loathing, and my soul needed someone who would remind me every day of the journey I was on. He treated me the way I was treating myself: self-abuse, disrespect, not worthy, of very little value.

My emotional state of self-loathing was a match for Rudi, who was also on the same level of spiritual growth. Self-loathing people behave in destructive, abusive, disrespectful and many other negative ways. A person cannot show love if he or she does not have love inside for themselves. A person views the world through their spiritual and emotional state. A self-loathing couple will create a toxic, abusive relationship until one or both of the partners outgrow the other and will then separate and transcend the relationship.

Rudi was a teacher who came to support me on my journey towards self-love.

Rune was an angel who came to show me my beauty and perfection, but I hadn't grown to the level where I could recognise the love he was offering, as my context for love at the time was that it came with abuse and had to be earned.

RECESSION

THE BUSINESS HAD GROWN EXPONENTIALLY and my suppliers and stock had increased dramatically with the upgrade of my merchandise. But with my five outlets in some of the busiest areas in Cape Town I had no difficulty in moving these volumes of stock until the recession hit in 1990s It was as if the consumer train had completely stopped. The turnover of my business plummeted by more than 50%, and I was in financial trouble because I couldn't meet my overheads, let alone pay my creditors.

Although I had trouble meeting payment terms, I was in constant communication with my suppliers, with whom I had developed a good working relationship. Most of my suppliers extended my terms as they trusted me, and it was in their interests to weather this storm with me so they could get their money at the end of the day. I knew if just one of them handed me over, the others would panic and I would go into liquidation, which was something I was trying to avoid at all cost.

I was fighting to keep my company afloat and was hoping to trade myself out of my financial woes. I was devastated when I received the first summons from one of my main suppliers and went into panic mode. I was stressed out, and my eyes were pussy, with the result that I could hardly see through them. I developed a twitch on one side of my face and feared a stroke was close.

Cat was living with me at my big house on the Lake and at the time she was seeing a lovely man by the name of Jim who has since passed on. Jim was quite a character and lived a fast life, but he had a big heart and only wanted to help others. He saw the stress I was under and came up with a suggestion. His bright idea was that he would burn my factory down to the ground and I could claim the R7-million insurance money. At first, I thought he was insane and laughed at this, but after mulling it over in my mind it seemed like a good plan and in my desperation I ditched my values and integrity.

I agreed and everything was planned for the following Friday evening. Although I had been instructed to go out as an alibi, and not stress at home, I was extremely anxious when I realised the seriousness of what was about to happen. I was at war within myself. I imagined the worst-case scenario of getting caught and landing up in prison. On the other hand, the relief of being able to pay everyone and save my company was greater than my fears.

Jim had rounded up a few of his friends and after dark they went into operation. While they were busy pouring petrol on the adjacent field and lighting the match, my neighbour across the road, who was also a good friend, spotted them and decided to play hero and apprehend them. He fired a few shots into the air and Jim and his friends scattered in different directions as they ran for their lives. My neighbour notified the police who were at the scene within minutes and called me to meet them at my shop. Although I was incensed by his interference, I pretended to be immensely grateful for his assistance.

I eventually traded myself out of my cash flow problems and in hindsight was very relieved that the fire operation had failed.

STRESS OF BUSINESS

I WAS COMPLETELY OVERWHELMED BY trying to cope with five huge Curtain Warehouse outlets spread across Cape Town, as well as managing a property rental company, which at this stage had grown to a sizable portfolio with more than twenty tenants in various apartments and houses. As long as my kids were taken care of, I had no time to worry about my personal life.

Because of my prolonged stress, I contracted shingles, a form of herpes that causes severe pain under the skin. My doctor prescribed very strong antibiotics for me to clear the condition and I didn't realise that antibiotics often render the contraceptive pill ineffective. I had never missed a period for any other reason in the past, other than when I was pregnant, and this time I had missed my period twice and had started to feel very strange. I told Rudi and with the boys we went to the family doctor, who confirmed the pregnancy. I broke down and cried, and for one second considered having an abortion. However, when I told the boys, they both promised to help me take care of the baby.

Rudi was still living with his mother and only visited a few times a week. I heard rumours again that he had been seen with the same gym woman in various public places. When I challenged him on it, he did not deny it but instead asked me if I would accept a second wife in my life. I was dumbfounded, looked at him as if I were the one who had gone crazy, and physically threw him out of my house.

His parents were ecstatic that he was seeing a 'decent' Muslim woman and they were very impressed that she came from a well-known family within the Muslim community. A few months into my pregnancy, I received a note from his mother addressing me as "Lizard". It read: - "Leave my son alone as he is happy with his new girlfriend and the baby you're carrying is not his. Go look for the father."

LEAVING THE DREAM HOME

WHILE PREGNANT WITH MY THIRD child and with two younger children dependent on me, I could no longer manage the upkeep of my house and as a result had to move out of my dream home. It was too large, and it held too many painful memories for me to maintain it. I began searching for a house closer to my children's school in Constantia. I saw an advertisement for a house to be auctioned in Bergvliet and, with my seven-month pregnant bulge, I went to the auction alone and was the highest bidder, as I was determined to settle my kids into their new home before I delivered my baby.

Rudi decided at this time to go on a pilgrimage to Mecca and he did not come to me or my children to inform us that he was leaving. He simply disappeared and returned to us three months later when I was in hospital suffering from stress and severe heart palpitations. He never visited me or showed any concern for my condition. While I was in my last trimester of pregnancy, a few of my friends told me they had received an invitation to Rudi's wedding at the Alphen Hotel. On a Saturday morning, a regular customer and friend came into the shop and reminded me of the wedding which was taking place as we spoke. I broke down. I went to lie under one of the fabric tables. I didn't want anyone to see my humiliation and pain.

Rudi and Zea got married at the Alphen Hotel without informing me or my children of his decision to take another wife. It was as if we did not exist. The day after the wedding, I heard a knock on the door and I opened up to find Rudi standing on the step with a box of leftover food from the wedding. Insulted and outraged, I threw him off my property.

When I went to pay my respects on the day his father passed away, along with my huge bulge, I saw Zea, who was also pregnant, which explained why the marriage was so rushed. The pain of Rudi fathering a child with another woman was so deep that it shattered me more than any previous affair he had had.

I was able to maintain the façade of someone in control during the day at work and in front of my children, but at night, alone in my bed, I allowed myself to be overcome by sadness and heartache. My uncontrollable sobs almost choked me as I struggled to breathe. Darkness and pain seemed to have become my life.

On the day that I was to have a caesarean section, Rudi had committed to attend Sammy's birth, but he didn't appear, so my sister Cat sat in and witnessed Sammy's birth instead. Having gone through a third pregnancy alone, I was at my lowest point - vulnerable and sad. There was no strength left in me to fight, and I felt more alone and unloved than ever before.

Despite being in a lot of pain, I had no intention of hurting myself.

Insight:
The rejection and disregard Rudi showed towards me highlighted the fact that I was not valued as a person. It confirmed that, no matter how much I had achieved materially, I was still not "worthy".

HIV AIDS

WHEN I RETURNED TO MY business three weeks after the birth of my daughter, Sammy, I found a huge pile of unopened letters on my desk. I opened one after the other, mostly statements from companies. Then I opened one letter from the insurance company which shook my world. The words jumped out at me: "We have declined your insurance policy due to your medical report. Contact your doctor immediately."

I froze. I sat horrified as confused and scary thoughts raced through my mind. I imagined the worst! Panic-stricken, I jumped up, ran down the stairs to my car, and raced to my doctor and friend who ushered me into his consulting room. He took a medical form with results from my folder and proceeded to read the HIV results as "reactive", which he explained to be neither positive nor negative but usually the first phase of a positive result.

I have always viewed HIV more as a shameful curse, rather than a death sentence. I was ashamed of the embarrassment that this disease would cause my children and my family.

It was at this point that I stopped listening to my doctor. As fear and anxiety gripped my chest, I started heaving as I struggled to get air into my lungs. I stared blankly at the doctor, trying to speak, but words eluded me. There were no words, just a million questions raced through my mind as I tried to come to terms with the reality of contracting HIV and its potentially horrific consequences.

My mind raced to the future, picturing the life of a mother living with HIV, and I thought of my lovely daughter, who might also have the disease. I even thought of Rudi's new wife and their baby, who could have it too. As shame and guilt clouded my judgement, I started berating myself for putting my family in this embarrassing situation. The doctor told me to return in two weeks for a retest as he walked me to the car. I sat in the driver's seat for a long time, pondering life as I slowly started the car. Suddenly, I looked up into the sky and the clouds seemed more beautiful than I'd ever seen before.

Upon returning home, I sat under my fig tree as the sun beckoned, comforting me with its rays, and for the first time I was able to see the beauty of nature - the trees, the sky, the birds, my children. For the first time I began to appreciate how precious and beautiful life is, and how fortunate I was that I was still alive. Solly came to sit with me and, as much as I wished to keep my status secret from my children, I felt compelled to share this with him as, at sixteen, he was now all grown up and had become my friend and support.

He sat quietly and listened, thereafter sharing with me his knowledge of this shameful disease as he had just completed a thesis at school. He did not judge me; he only sat and comforted me. As much as I was panic-stricken, I had somehow woken up to the universe and for the first time I was not focusing on my pain but my blessings, on the gift of life itself! For the first time I lived fully, taking in all the beauty that, up to this point, I had taken for granted.

After two days of moving around in a daze, the suspense of not knowing was killing me, and I knew I couldn't wait for another two weeks for the results. I called the doctor and asked if there was any way we could do a quick test to get the results earlier.

HIV was the manifestation of the shame I was carrying and not valuing myself. I'd attracted this wake-up call! It made me realise how precious and beautiful the gift of life is!

He told me of a test called the Western Blot which was quite expensive but 99% accurate and results were available within forty-eight hours. The Western Blot test separates the blood proteins and detects the specific proteins (called HIV antibodies) that indicate an HIV infection.

I rushed to have this test done. The wait dragged on, and feelings ranging from shame, guilt and panic, to acceptance, appreciation and trust yo-yoed inside me. It brought me to the realisation that life was indeed for living and loving and nothing else mattered.

When my doctor finally gave me the results it was even more confusing, as the HIV tests came back negative, but they revealed that there was something else hovering in my body. They suspected leukaemia, as I had more white blood cells than red. After many more painful tests, the upshot was that I was as healthy as a horse, which was good news, but even better news was my renewed appreciation and excitement for life itself.

I still did not realise or acknowledge how powerful and special I was. I was still in awe of the Higher Power!

Waldorf had been the perfect school for my sons, offering alternative teaching, handling each child as an individual. Rudolf Steiner, the founder of the anthroposophy movement, believed the school should "receive children in reverence, educate them in love and let them go forth in freedom," which was a far cry from the traditional government education. However, the tension and upheaval had finally taken its toll with Solly who was not coping with his final school year, so when my son chose to live with his father it was the last betrayal; it was too much to bear. I sank to new depths. This was my baby, the child I had protected with my life, who was now turning his back on me. I felt defeated. In my eyes, Rudi had won.

THE SEYCHELLES

ALL THE EMOTIONAL TRAUMA I had suffered over the past years took its toll on me and I was in a very fragile and vulnerable space. I needed to heal to take care of myself and my children, and I decided to physically go away to a different place where I would not have contact with Rudi or my familiar environment. I did not have the energy and strength to handle the responsibility of staff and shops. I knew that I wasn't in a healthy state to be a fit mother or employer and I decided to pack up home and go and live in the Seychelles for as long as was necessary to heal. I had previously met a lady in my shop from the Seychelles and had kept in contact with her. She agreed to meet me on my arrival and promised to help me find accommodation and to settle into my new home.

I made the reservations for the three of us, as Solly was now living with his father and new family. Harry's teacher was surprised but agreed with the idea of him taking an extended holiday as he believed it would do us all good to have a temporary change. He had seen Harry become very withdrawn and assured me that Harry was an intelligent child who would be capable of picking up missed lessons on his return, but that I should continue with private tutoring of maths on the island. I didn't inform Rudi of my decision, as I feared he might have tried to stop us from leaving. He was still lifting Harry to school every day, but on the morning of our departure Harry told his father he wasn't feeling well.

Our departure time from Cape Town to Johannesburg was scheduled for 1pm and I still had an entire three-bedroom house with furniture, clothes, toys and so on to move into storage. The moment Rudi drove out the driveway, my friends arrived. They worked swiftly wrapping, packing and boxing crockery and valuables as the guys were loading it all into hired trucks.

By 11am I had handed the keys to the new tenant and had enough time at the airport to put 250 kilograms of excess luggage on cargo to arrive on the same flight in Johannesburg. I was off with my 10-year-old son and my six-month-old daughter to carve out a new life in a new country.

When I arrived at Johannesburg airport, I had two hours in which to clear the excess cargo and I left Harry with Sammy while I took a taxi to the cargo terminal. There was a long queue for cargo clearances. I realised that if I was going to wait in that queue, I was going to miss my flight and ran behind the counters to the shelves and started pulling out my goods with the permission of the clerks. I rushed back to the main terminal, where I found Harry sitting on the floor, holding my sleeping baby in front of the check-in counter. The clerk felt extremely sorry for us and checked in all my 250kg excess baggage at no extra cost.

With a sigh of great relief, I finally settled into my seat, closed my eyes as my feelings of angst were replaced by a sense of triumph and satisfaction, knowing that a new life awaited me.

ISLAND LIFE

THE SEYCHELLES ARCHIPELAGO CONSISTS OF over one hundred islands, situated in the Indian Ocean rim, many of which have been dedicated as national nature reserves. The majestic shores are fringed with white sand, palm trees and granite boulders – it is paradise. The main island, Mahé, is dotted with luxury resorts and hotels and tourists use it as their base to island-hop.

We arrived late evening in the Seychelles, where we were welcomed by island music with exotic ladies in brightly coloured flowing skirts dancing the local Sega dance, celebrating joy and liveliness. I was filled with excitement and exhilaration and was keen to start my new life in this paradise, which I had visited only a few times previously, although I had always intended to return. My newfound friend was there waiting with the three taxis she had hired to transport all our luggage and as we stepped out of the terminal building the tropical heat and humidity enveloped me in a loving embrace. I was home.

We arrived in convoy at the Casuarina Hotel, where the boxes of disposable nappies, Jungle Oats, coffee, peanut butter and other foodstuffs and clothing were stacked up to the ceiling and filled the entire room, leaving only the beds exposed.

The following morning, sitting on my balcony overlooking the sea and breathing in the clean fresh air, I felt like I'd just escaped from prison. Freedom stared me in the eyes; contentment seeped through my veins as we sat eating croissants and drinking coffee. I scanned the newspapers for a home to rent but it was in French, so my friend assisted in finding a semi-detached two-bedroom house to rent on the golf estate opposite the Reef Hotel.

Our new life had begun, but Harry was very sad and cried for his dad for the first week as the two of us sat sipping our drinks watching the full moon over the ocean. I knew this was the perfect place to heal as a family.

I hired a nanny for Sammy, found a maths tutor for Harry, and hired an open-topped blue beach buggy. Life seemed perfect! Our idyllic life took off as Harry started making friends with the local boys. He was the only boy in the area with a soccer ball, which made him the most popular boy in the vicinity. Boys were constantly bringing gifts of the fruit that was growing everywhere on the island, just to be part of Harry's soccer team. I planned a daily program for him, which included time in the library, where we soaked up knowledge on subjects that fascinated me, such as Greek Mythology, Egyptology and geographical formations, in between his maths lessons.

I made friends with some of the local ladies and spent plenty of time lying on the beach during the day and learning to do the Sega dance at night on the local hotel dance floor. My family began to feel secure, participating in communal functions and making friends easily with the warm-hearted local Seychellois.

I got to know my way around the island and learnt that the fun side was on the northern part of the island, particularly the Beau Vallon Bay Hotel, which is where I went on weekly outings, spending lazy days on the beach surrounded by wealthy tourists.

On one of these occasions, I met the manager of the hotel, a German man called Lothar. We became friends and he extended an open invitation to us to spend as much time as we wanted at his hotel and this is where I met many important people, such as the prince of Kuwait and others. All sadness was momentarily forgotten as I joined in the fun, Sega dancing the night away on the beach under the warm starlit sky. It was idyllic, a life so simple and stress-free, exactly what my soul needed to heal.

After a few weeks, Solly arrived to spend the school holidays, laden with boxes of treats and niceties from his dad, and inside one of these boxes was a letter addressed to me. As I read the words of his undying love for me and my children and the grave mistake he had made in marrying Zea, begging me to come home, I saw red! I promptly put the letter back into the envelope and forwarded the letter to his wife in South Africa.

Aunty Kay, Jenny and her three children arrived from South Africa and my two-bedroom cottage was filled to capacity but it was fun to have friends from home who kept us busy exploring Mahe and some of the surrounding islands, where we went scuba diving, cycling, sailing, parachuting and partying the night away at the various tourist hotels. We explored the spice routes, the famous botanical gardens and visited the local markets, sampling local creole specialities and delicacies.

JOB HUNTING

AFTER SOLLY AND AUNT KAY left, things seemed less fun and I became bored with the continuous idleness, itching to get back to work and get my teeth into something. I canvassed the various hotels to see if I could do business with them. I heard via the grapevine that the Miss World Pageant was taking place at the Plantation Hotel and decided to visit the hotel to see if I could get some interior decorating work.

On the agreed day for our trip to the opposite end of the Island, Jenny and I settled the younger kids into the beach buggy, with the older kids taking public transport, and set off on our long journey through the only treacherous volcanic road with runs across the island from east to west. An hour later, I finally parked my car in the parking area of the hotel. We left the kids at the pool, and I went to wait outside the French manager's office, hoping to see him without an appointment. I sat there for the entire day, only leaving to go to the toilet, until after 5pm, when his secretary informed me that he couldn't see me that day. I left but was determined to return the following day, when again I took up residence in the same chair as before.

He saw me for ten minutes late in the afternoon and I took full advantage of it. I was armed with fabric sample books that my staff had sent from South Africa. He liked one of the fabrics, but the colour was wrong. I promised him that I will find the perfect fabric for his 400 rooms with all the public areas to be completely refurbished. It was the biggest contract I had ever quoted on, and I was hungry for it. My adrenalin was pumping;

I was back to my confident self and was determined to get this contract by hook or by crook.

A few days later I excitedly packed up our remaining stuff, handed the house keys back to the owner, and set off back to Cape Town to source the fabric for this contract. I couldn't find exactly what he was looking for and decided to design the perfect fabric in the appropriate colours. Cat and I were back on the plane a week later with the new designs in hand to present to the manager. He loved the new designs but, after I gave him the quotation, he needed time to consult with his superiors, which he said might take a few days.

SUCCESS LEADS TO NEW BUSINESS

IT WAS A TOUGH BIDDING process, and the waiting and uncertainty were excruciating as I anxiously whiled away the time on the island, not knowing when to schedule my return to Cape Town. But then my trust in God would come and strengthen my faith, reminding me again of how far I had come.

A week later, the manager came back with acceptance of the quotation. I was elated and my exhilaration knew no bounds. I was giddy with excitement on the plane back to Cape Town and couldn't wait to share the news with my family and staff. It was undoubtedly one of my greatest achievements thus far.

My team, which included some of my family members, worked night and day to fulfil the contract in the short time before the scheduled departure date of the cargo vessel. A few of my staff members were already in the Seychelles, awaiting the arrival of the container while they were busy preparing for the refurbishment

The hotel started filling up with the arrivals of celebrities, judges and beauty queens. A fleet of helicopters arrived, bringing wealthy Emirates businessmen, who pitched their marque palaces, adorned with chandeliers and Persian rugs, on the grass. The band UB40 entertained them on a private beach close to the hotel, where some of the pageant girls became familiar with the dignitaries from Dubai. It was another world, far removed from the one I knew.

When the ship arrived and unloaded, the team got busy, frantically unpacking, measuring, fitting, until the rooms and public areas were transformed from dark and depressing, to bright and glamorous. I was proud of my team, who were completely dedicated and worked tirelessly until every inch of the resort was perfectly completed. The hotel was transformed into a tropical paradise with colours ranging from green, yellows and turquoise on beautiful textured fabrics.

The guests loved the interiors, and this project paved the way for many similar ventures to come.

I never intended to live in Seychelles for the rest of my life. It was just a stopgap and a means to recovery. To return to South Africa well enough to carry on with my life, I had to rejuvenate and heal. I did not intend to open a business in the Seychelles; it was too quiet for my overactive mind. The pace was too slow.

FURNTEX

WHEN I RETURNED TO SOUTH Africa, I was motivated to start designing my own ranges of textiles and wallpapers on the back of my Seychelles success, and my wholesale company Furntex was born. I so enjoyed working with designs and my passion for colour worked in my favour. My fabric sample books were displayed in many décor shops around the country, and I supplied many decorators with exclusive fabrics.

I was surprised at how fast my business grew. No business plan, no feasibility studies, no fancy methods - just hard work and a relentless drive to improve, to reach the top. This spurred me on to create my own range in South Africa.

When I'd designed the two designs for the Miss World Pageant, I'd printed extra fabric for my shops and it was an instant bestseller. I had always been passionate about colours, the ambiance they create and the meaning behind each colour. Mixing colours in designs was more a hobby than a career. When I was designing or searching for design ideas it was always motivated by an emotion. I wanted to create vibrant coloured fabric to uplift and inspire joy when you entered a room.

The first local range I designed for my wholesale company Furntex was called Tropicana, which had the Seychelles hotel design in it as well. I bought a few designs from a design studio at the Heimtextil exhibition in German and one of those was called Seahorses, which became my bestseller. I printed this range with a company whose head offices were in Pretoria. The representative was a guy called Jay Bark, who had been in the home fabric industry all his life and knew fabrics very well. His children all had their own fabric outlets and agencies.

Jay was a very amiable man with many years' experience in the home textile industry and I trusted him implicitly. That's why I decided to print with his company instead of some of the bigger ones. We couldn't keep up with the demand for the seahorse fabric and repeated the 1000-metre order many times.

One particular day, as I passed a shop in the Access Park discount shopping complex in Kenilworth, I froze as I looked at the fabrics displayed in the window. It was my seahorse design printed in different colours. The shop belonged to Jay's daughter-in-law!

I was livid and dialled Jay's number on my mobile from outside the shop. He answered with his usual friendliness. I exploded. "Jay, what's my design doing in your daughter's shop in different colours?"

He was calm and replied, "Liz, let's sit down and discuss it calmly in your office tomorrow". I was even more outraged at his nonchalant attitude. He had just stolen my hard work, my pride from my first range.

"No, I want answers now!" I blurted out.

He met me and told me his factory had decided to print my design in different colours and he had been told to distribute it. I was dumbstruck. It was bizarre how a factory could copy a design that belonged to someone else.

COURT CASE

I WAS EVEN MORE INFURIATED when Jay claimed that I had given them permission. I got into my car and went to see the best copyright lawyers in town, Adams and Adams in the city centre.

The case dragged on for months with them sticking to their story and meanwhile selling their fabric much cheaper than mine. The lawyers' costs were exorbitant and I had already spent R250 000 with them, but I wasn't going to back down. This was David going up against Goliath! A court date was set for us to appear in the High Court in Pretoria.

I was relieved when I learnt that I was to be accompanied by a female lawyer with whom I had been dealing from the Cape Town office. On arrival in Johannesburg, we were met by the driver from their Pretoria office who checked us into the Sandton Sun Hotel. I felt secure knowing that my lawyer was in the room adjacent to mine. After we had settled in, we were taken to meet with our advocate in his chambers to go over all the details of the case, as we were appearing first thing the following morning.

I hardly slept from sheer anxiety. It was my first time in the High Court and I was scared.

Walking into court the following morning and facing my opposition was nerve-wracking. There was Jay, the once friendly and kind man I'd got to know and trust, who was now my sworn enemy and made himself out to be the puppet of his company, controlled by his superiors.

His legal team consisted of three fierce-looking giant Afrikaans men, who verbally threatened and intimidated me. While I was terrified of them, I put on a brave face and wouldn't let them see my fear because they could use it against me. It wasn't until I got to my hotel room that I could finally breathe and relax with a glass of wine.

It had been an exhausting day, where we spent hours and hours being questioned over and over, with Jay lying and me trying to prove that I was the legal owner of the design. The whole legal pantomime had taken its toll on me. By the third morning, having not slept for almost three nights, I was ready to pass out. I couldn't move a limb, couldn't even get a word out. I was totally spent: mentally, emotionally and physically. I just wanted to get to my bed in Cape Town to bury myself under the blankets. Besides the exhaustion of the courtroom where we spent all day, there was the fear of being attacked in my hotel by these men who openly showed hostility and made threats towards me. When the court finally ruled in my favour, I was triumphant and returned to Cape Town victorious and stronger for the experience.

NEXT LEVEL

I FELT LIKE I HAD reached a new level in my business, as I was no longer just a job buyer of redundant and seconded merchandise, but was one of the sought after designers with my own fabric ranges. I started travelling the world again to attend textile fairs and expos, this time not as a buyer but as an exhibitor. I displayed my designs at the big expos such as Heimtextil in Frankfurt, Germany, in New York and many other countries, who bought my designs.

The Miss World Pageant project had galvanised my talents and inspired me to use the new company to push into the rest of Africa. I continued to source ranges from Germany, Italy and other parts of Europe and employed Amina to manage Furntex, now housed in offices above the Curtain Warehouse. My sample fabric books were on the shelves of decorating shops everywhere. I was landing contracts from the government and many smaller local hotels, even supplying big hotels such as the Table Bay Hotel in Cape Town.

Besides my successful fabric business, my property business grew into an empire. I had become a very wealthy, successful and confident woman. The world was my oyster, and I was flying high. I had since moved into a mansion in Constantia, which I'd bought as a small house on a big plot and, as usual, I'd started renovating until I was now living in a five-bedroomed mansion with both my sons enjoying their own apartment on the property.

I entertained and lived on a whole new level. Hiring a private plane in Australia to fly my family to visit a remote island that was for sale was no big deal. I attended antique jewellery auctions and bought precious jewellery, which stayed locked up in my safe until it was all stolen.

Living in Constantia in a mansion needed constant maintenance, so I employed a full-time gardener, two housekeepers and a cook. Money was not a problem- it was just flowing in – but it was the constant juggling of responsibilities that was exhausting. As a result, I did not spend enough time with my loved ones. I started to resent the continuous travelling and time I was wasting sitting in airport lounges and on planes.

The money gave me a false sense of power as I was treated like a queen everywhere I went. My luxury cars and air of confidence demanded respect and adoration.

PEDDLARS ON THE BEND

ONE NIGHT AFTER WORK, MY sister Cat and her friend Jenny suggested we go across the street to the local sports bar and restaurant, Peddlars on the Bend.

As we entered, we spotted one of our regular wealthy German customers of Curtain Warehouse. She was sitting amidst a group of men, one of whom was her husband. As soon as she saw us, she left her companions and came to greet us, inviting us to join them. She asked for a table big enough for ten people, and a tall, large-framed man with the sharpest blue eyes arranged the seating, placing me across the table from him, where he continued to stare into my eyes, amused at my visible discomfort.

His air of confidence indicated that he was clearly the leader of the group, as everyone at the table seemed to defer to him with the utmost respect, treating him like a god. He introduced himself as Dr Karl Heinz and told me that he was in Cape Town to play golf with his golfing buddies, whom he had brought along with him from Germany, and that he owned a house on the famous Steenberg golf estate.

One of his friends owned his own helicopter company in Germany, but Karl had paid him handsomely to accompany him to Cape Town to fly him around in his private helicopter.

I disliked Karl immediately because of his arrogance. He reminded me of my childhood, when people were treated differently based on their colour and their wealth!

However, he was clearly enamoured of me and invited me to join him for lunch the following day, but I refused due to my business duties. However, we joined him for dinner at a restaurant on the Uitsig wine farm the following night. Over dinner he made it very clear that he was interested in me and he invited me on a shopping spree the following day. Even though I wasn't in love with Karl, I felt flattered by the attention of such an important and distinguished man who demanded respect.

SPOILT ROTTEN

AT 9AM THE FOLLOWING MORNING, the chauffeur was at my door collecting me in a black Mercedes limo, where Karl was waiting in the back seat. Jenny and Ava joined us as we took the highway to Cavendish Square, an upmarket shopping mall. We visited many exclusive boutiques where Karl would take a seat while I would parade around in the many beautiful outfits the shop assistants brought to me. I looked good in most of them because of my tall slender shape, and for the first time I didn't look at the price tag. Karl would nod his head to give approval for an outfit and this item would be added to the fast-growing pile of designer clothes he had already bought me.

Heavily laden with paper bags full of designer clothes, we hit the jewellery shops, where he selected several gold rings and an hour later I left with three beautiful rings, each one more exquisite than the next, littered with platinum and diamonds, gold with big rubies inlaid and a plaited gold and platinum band. He also bought me a limited-edition gold Cartier watch.

The entire day seemed like a scene from the movie, *Pretty Woman*. Karl loved entertaining and my sisters and friends were constant dinner companions at some of the finest restaurants in the Cape, pairing some of the best wines with gourmet food prepared by celebrated chefs. His pilot would fly us to dine at restaurants in the winelands, and we even spent some time on the golf estate in George.

When he left to return to Germany, he handed me the keys of his house on the golf estate and placed his chauffeur and housekeeper at my disposal. His cellar was stacked with some of the best wine from all over the world. It was fun, entertaining my friends on such a grand scale.

When I left to exhibit at Heimtextil in Germany, I was privileged to sit next to him in first class on Lufthansa, where he was a well-known traveller and seat no. 3 was always reserved for him. We were chauffeur-driven wherever we went, and we shopped in the most exclusive boutiques in Europe.

I was constantly accompanied by my two younger sisters, as Karl enjoyed having an entourage wherever we went. Karl and I were flown in his private helicopter to the most exclusive hotel and spa in the Black Forest, where we were treated like royalty as the waiters wheeled the most delectable canapes and aperitifs into our lounge as we entertained some of his wealthy friends in our private suite.

This was a fantasy world and it felt like I was the main character in a fairy tale, where every wish was my command.

However, I started to be less enamoured with the money and the fancy clothes as I found that, after the initial excitement and all the attention, it all seemed meaningless. I felt that I was selling myself for money and it made me feel degraded and as if I had let myself down. I was successful in my own right, and I enjoyed making my own money and loved what I was doing.

I also realised that Karl was very serious about me romantically. Then the day came when he proposed to me. He had invited me to a restaurant alone and I knew something serious was coming as we were always surrounded by many people. Sitting across from him, I could tell he had something important on his mind and his words threw me off balance.

"Liz, I love you. Will you marry me?"

With utmost compassion I replied, "Karl, I am not in love with you and it would not be right for me to marry you".

Although I didn't want to be owned, I never believed that he was in love with me because I didn't believe a man could love me. I always assumed they had a hidden agenda. "If they knew who I was, they would run." I couldn't allow anyone to see the shame, the ugly, the not good enough, the not worthy. The façade I had built was my protection against rejection and pain, which meant I did not show any weakness. Being vulnerable was my greatest fear!

I declined his proposal and bid him a very fond but sad farewell.

Five years later, after he got his inheritance of Euro 200-million, he called me from Germany and again asked for me to reconsider his proposal and I told him I would give him an answer the following day, but I turned my phone off. He never contacted me again.

Insight:
Karl spoiling me with his money was his way of showing me how much he valued me, and how worthy I am! I could not see what he saw in me because I was still in a spiritual state of self-loathing and shame. Due to this, I was suspicious of him, believing he had other motives besides loving me.

SOULMATE

UPON SETTLING INTO THE FIVE-STAR hotel close to the Heimtextil, where Karl insisted we stay after he'd scoffed at the three-star hotel my secretary had booked us into, was a privilege. Having a room in a fancy hotel so close to the exhibition hall does not just require lots of money, it is reserved only for a few VIP regulars and Karl was certainly one of them, and price was not an issue.

I was excited to have my two sisters accompany me on this annual trip, which I'd used to make alone since I had decided to trade in the international textile arena.

Having dressed up in our finest suits, we made our way to the fair, which was within walking distance. It was the first day of the annual textile exhibition and the excitement amongst the crowd of well-dressed people who had travelled from across the globe, queuing to get their three-day entrance pass, was palpable. I was equally excited and privileged to be part of this event as this expo was where the top textile manufacturing companies showcased their latest ranges of designs and colours, woven or printed on the most sumptuous and luxurious textiles.

As usual, the size of that expo venue was overwhelming and, as in previous years, I confined my visit to only the exhibition halls that were related to my line of business.

I was like a child in a candy store surrounded by so many beautiful fabrics and as we strolled past one stand more elaborately decorated than the last, I suddenly stopped as the most magnificent piece of fabric loosely draped around a marble pillar caught my eye. A large crowd of people were blocking the entrance to the stand as they all stopped to admire this display. It was a showstopper! As my eyes scanned over the rest of the stand I suddenly looked into a pair of piercing black eyes. I stood riveted to the spot and, as if in a trance, I walked like a zombie towards the eyes and came to a stop in front of a man who was talking to two customers facing him. I was completely oblivious to my surroundings because I had been captured by his intense and expressive eyes that seemed to draw me into his very soul. I had no control over my actions and there were no thoughts. It was as if something or someone else had taken over my being.

I stood there, looking down at him, and my entire body started shaking violently. He stared at me in shocked recognition and his hands were shaking. He could not control it either; he was visibly shaken. I could not utter a word as I slowly lowered myself to occupy one of the vacant chairs. No words were spoken. We just stared at one another as if we knew! We were unaware of anyone or anything around us. It was as if only we existed! Both of us were in a trance, as if we were in another realm or another lifetime. Our confusion was mutual, but the connection between us was so strong that it engulfed us. We tried to figure it out, but it made no sense. It felt as if we had known each other for eons. The entire incident was inexplicable.

Bewildered at what had transpired, Cat anxiously asked if I was okay; I was not. After a while, he managed to introduce himself as Reg and asked us to join him and some colleagues for dinner. Disorientated, I stood up and took my leave. I was completely baffled by the uncanny incident and I shared this with my sisters who told me I looked like I'd seen a ghost.

My reaction to seeing him again at the restaurant was no different and I spoke incoherently to the waiter who was waiting on my order, but I felt too bewildered to eat. It was most definitely a soul connection, and the entire episode was surreal.

The attraction we felt for each other was profound! The intensity of the emotions I felt for him made me giddy; it was euphoric! For the first time in my life there was no need for pretence, insecurities or self-consciousness, only feelings of bliss and happiness, which left me speechless.

The evening was perfect. As we spent the evening getting to know each other, I realised what unconditional love was all about. We saw each other again the following day and then it was time to bid each other goodbye!

Walking away from him felt like I was leaving half of myself behind. The deep raw pain I felt transmuted into an intense longing to see him again. I could not forget him. He was my constant companion in my fantasies at night. We had no contact with each other, as we knew our love was not about hurting others, especially our loved ones.

The following year I was invited to attend the very prestigious expo on Lake Como and would not have missed it for the world. Cat and Jenny accompanied me to this special place, which is the playground of the rich and famous.

The first day at these international expos is always the most exciting day as the opening celebrations are often a splendid occasion. This one was probably the most elaborate of them all, as we listened to the Italian orchestra playing to the tune of one the famous Italian opera singers in a 100-year-old Grand Castello on the lake. The interiors have been well preserved, with magnificent antique handwoven tapestries lining the walls, large ornate crystal and brass chandeliers hanging low from the five-metre-high ceilings, which boast beautiful murals and mouldings from time gone by. The thick red woollen carpets covering the floors still look as opulent as it did a century ago.

As with so many of the historical villas and castles in Italy that have become heritage sites, the Castello is now being used as a grand venue for functions such as weddings, conferences and expos. The ballroom was abuzz with activity, as the waiters made their rounds with large trays of a variety of cheeses, prosciutto and many other delectable antipasti accompanied by some of the finest prosecco.

The three of us were in our element as we socialised and flirted with the elite of the textile industry.

I sensed *him* before I saw *him* walking up the steps, coming into the ballroom where the celebrations were in full swing. My breath caught in my throat as I watched him enter the room. He stood out in the crowd with his tall muscular frame, which he carried gracefully as he walked across the room with an air of self-assurance. He was not handsome in a conventional way. Instead, his rugged bronze face showed a strong yet gentle character and when he smiled his warm eyes lit up, displaying modesty and humility. His crisp white shirt with a soft yellow tie and snugly fitted blue jeans screamed of confidence and style.

When he saw me, his eyes lit up with surprise and delight as he purposely strode towards me. My heart skipped a beat, my breathing quickened, and again I started shaking, this time stronger than the previous year. I almost dropped the glass I was holding as I struggled to control the involuntary shivering. As he stood there in front of me his eyes said it all: pure, unadulterated love poured forth, flooding my entire being.

Jenny and Cat quickly left us to join some of the new-found friends, and without saying a word he took my hand and led me out of the castle to sit on a bench overlooking the lake, where we once again got lost in each other's eyes.

He confessed to me how he had struggled to fit back into his normal life again after he said goodbye to me in Germany the previous year. He told me that he loved his wife and children and had never been tempted to enter into an extramarital affair, as he respected his marital vows and his commitment to his family. The connection between us had, however, created so much turmoil within him that he'd had great difficulty fitting back into the mould of the perfect life he had left behind before he went on his annual trip to Germany.

I admired him for his strong values, but it wasn't possible to love him even more than I already did. He told me that he loved me more than he had ever loved anyone else in his life and that I was certainly the love of his life. He invited me to dine with him at a very romantic palace on the lake.

I was ecstatic and took particular care with my dressing and donned my finest evening gown. The anticipation I felt at the thought of dining with him was exhilarating. When he fetched me from the villa where we were staying, in a chauffeur-driven black Mercedes, I could hardly contain my excitement. The sight of him looking debonair in a navy linen suit completed the fairy tale. Was I the princess in the fairy tale who'd met her prince? It certainly felt better than all the romantic novels I had ever read.

After the romantic dinner with this beautiful man, my soulmate, we decided to book into a room in this romantic palace. I was enraptured when we entered the room and a bouquet of red roses and tealight candles placed around the room were awaiting us. From the balcony we watched as the bright moonlight lit up the calm water of the lake, adding to the already perfect setting in celebration of our love as we slowly danced to the song *Endless Love* by Diana Ross.

The gentleness of his kiss and the tenderness in his eyes touched my very soul as the physical expression of our love ignited the flame inside of me, which up to that point had been lying dormant. I fell asleep knowing that I'd had a glimpse of heaven!

The following morning, as I slowly opened my eyes to the unfamiliar surroundings, it took a few seconds before the memory of the night before came flooding back, filling me with a warm radiance. I instinctively reached for him, but the bed was empty. Instead there was a note.

It read: "Liz, my darling, I love you more than I've ever loved another woman, but I have a family to whom I am committed. If only I had met you before I met my wife, I would have wanted to spend my life with you. You are my true love, and I will carry you around in my heart, always! Goodbye, R

And he was gone…

My heart felt like it had been ripped from my chest. I felt empty…

The trip on the lake no longer interested me.

I would have moved my world for him if he had asked!

Getting over the longing to be with him took a long time, but I knew our journey was complete! I knew in my soul that we must've been together in one of our previous lives. He left me with a memory so precious I will carry it with me to my grave and beyond.

Insight:

He gave me a gift of love so pure and beautiful; it completely changed my perception of love! Only now do I grasp the fact that, when I love others, I'm in reality loving myself because I'm feeling the emotion, not the other person. This knowledge has freed me from the notion that love must be reciprocated. I now see that loving someone or something benefits me and my entire community as the energy and vibration I exude affects others.

SAMMY

SAMMY, BEING THE BABY IN the household and much younger than her older brothers, had a hard time being heard. She usually hid in her room, not wanting to make an appearance since she was too shy.

Solly treated her as if she were his child and unwittingly passed his insecurities about his body, which he'd inherited from watching his father always dieting and my unhealthy relationship with food, onto Sammy. He constantly reminded her when she was eating too much, or the wrong food stuff, with the result that she became obsessed with food and became a plump little girl, which made her feel extremely insecure and unhappy at school.

Rudi was a compulsive eater and had a lifelong struggle with his weight, which fluctuated between 90 and 130 kilograms. Try as he might, none of the diets worked. He went to extreme lengths to lose weight such as having his teeth tied together, then a gastric bypass, amongst other drastic measures.

In addition to Solly monitoring Sammy's food intake, I also became aware that she ate too much and became a plump child at an early age. I became concerned about her weight when she was seven and attempted to curb her eating habits in many ways, notably by discouraging sweets.

One morning on my way to work, I heard an interview on the radio with an American author who had just published a book on weight loss. I was intrigued by her methods and rushed out to purchase the book. She believed you should only consume whatever food you are addicted to for breakfast, lunch and dinner, for as long as possible, until you become nauseous from eating it, so you won't desire or consume it again.

Excited to put this method to the test, I sent Solly and Sammy to Makro to buy all the sweets she loved, and they came back with a variety of Sammy's favourite sweets in a big brown box. With apprehension, she tore into the sweets, unable to believe the rationed treats were so readily available. As I watched her consume packet after packet for the first few days, I started doubting this method, since her appetite was not waning.

Soon, Solly was off to replenish the dwindling stocks. She had consumed in one week what she would normally have eaten over a few months and yet she was insatiable as she opened yet another packet.

I became increasingly concerned after a week that this tactic was not working, so I started spiking the sweets with Epsom salts, but it didn't deter her. When she realised they were spiked, she washed them under the tap and continued eating. I was at the end of this experiment as I feared this child was going to eat herself into a stupor, so I went back to rationing.

MOTHER'S DEATH

A FEW MONTHS LATER, JUST before my birthday in November 2000, I dropped my mother and two sisters off at Cape Town station, from where they caught the train to Gaborone to spend some time with Cat, who was living in Botswana with her boyfriend. I hugged her and waved them goodbye as I casually got back into my Mercedes, not knowing this would be the last time I would see my mother alive.

Unfortunately, Mom caught pneumonia while she was there. After leaving a restaurant one evening, she started coughing uncontrollably, collapsed and foamed at the mouth. She suffered a cardiac arrest lying on the floor of Cat's house and died later at the hospital. Sadly, I was not there to witness my mother's passing, and only saw her in a coffin when her body was flown back to Cape Town from Botswana.

My usual reaction was to go into deep shock, not being able to feel or cry, becoming numb, which was the default way I learned to defend myself from my childhood. In honour of my mother, I arranged a white funeral for her, which consisted of white flowers, a white casket and a white hearse. There was so much I wanted to say to her. My anger and judgement at her promiscuity and betrayal suddenly seemed so trivial in light of the great loss! She'd made sacrifices for her children without receiving any thanks or appreciation, yet she had loved and supported them unconditionally.

She was my anchor, my soft landing, my mentor! I couldn't imagine that this larger-than-life being was now a lifeless corpse. I'm still traumatised whenever I think of her in that white coffin; the image doesn't fit with my memories of her strength and courage. As a result of the death of my mother, everything in my life ceased to make sense to me, and I fell apart.

She was a fearless fighter and survivor in the face of the most painful situations and how she transcended it still inspires me to this day.

Insight:
I realised for the first time how special I was. I was the "love child"
they had both prayed for. I accepted that I was born from love and
not from shame!

THE LURE OF GRAND WEST

AFTER MY MOTHER'S PASSING, LIFE seemed to take on a different
meaning for me. I wanted to experience new things, live a
different life, so I moved out of my Constantia house and into one
of the Green Point apartments I owned and became part of Cape
Town's social scene. I still couldn't mourn. Instead, I became a
regular at the new Grand West Casino that had just opened its
doors in December 2000. It was the first official casino in Cape
Town. Before that, we'd had to spend lots of money to travel up
to Sun City on the northern outskirts of Johannesburg to enjoy
serious gambling.

As soon as I walked into this fantasy palace with its grand
décor of plush carpets, comfy leather couches with gold framed
mirrors lining the walls, all my troubles fell by the wayside and my
obsession with winning became the focal point of my existence.
Amidst the chiming of the machines and flickering lights, I
awaited the next spin, jackpot or win with heady excitement.

The VIP service I received as one of their big players added
to the attraction of the place. At a click of my fingers, my choice
of alcohol and food would appear. The invitations to their social
events kept me busy and this gambling universe became a way
of life for me. It was a magical world where my problems and

sadness were temporarily forgotten, to be replaced with shame and guilt in the aftermath. I spent hours, days, nights gambling to forget, and in doing so I lost millions of Rand.

To pay for my addiction, I stupidly started liquidating my assets. The slot machines became my companions. There I could forget my sadness and grief. This was the perfect escape, as there was no reason to think or interact. I did not have to deal with the loss of my mother. In fact, I wasn't dealing with anything besides waiting for the next jackpot or the next spin.

I would mostly go to the casino on my own. I wanted to get away from reality and I buried myself in this dark world where lies, alcohol and gambling went hand in hand, to be consumed by shame and guilt after huge losses or the exhilaration after a jackpot win. The highs and lows kept me hooked and nothing else in the world mattered. I was running so hard from experiencing my pain, instead of facing it. I was out of control and in the process of losing everything I had worked for: my businesses, my property and my family.

Insight:
The slot machines were my companion and filled the void of loneliness and sadness and temporarily masked the trauma and pain. The shame and guilt in the aftermath felt comfortable. I was shame and I did shameful things. The subsequent cycle of self-punishment perpetuated the addiction. Once I realised that the addiction was helping me get through the darkness, I accepted and embraced it and no longer needed it as a crutch.

SOLLY COMES OUT

IT WAS ON ONE OF these gambling sprees to Sun City, when I went with my two sisters and my children to live in the Palace Hotel, that I became suspicious that Solly was gay, as he seemed mesmerised by another young man in the disco, whom he later claimed he thought was a woman. When I confronted him, he denied it and I readily believed that my suspicions were unfounded. I was relieved to put this suspicion behind me.

A few weeks after our return from Sun City, he came into my room to tell me about his wild night out with his friends, and while listening I observed that he never once mentioned girls' names. I commented on this and, feeling caught out, he finally admitted that he was gay.

I wasn't surprised in the slightest, as deep inside I had always known the truth. However, his confession caught me off guard and I couldn't utter a word as the tears streamed down my cheeks, as sadness turned to grief. I cried for many hours alone in my bedroom until Harry finally came into the room to comfort me, assuring me that he would always protect his brother.

I mourned for many months. Wherever I went, I would have all the ladies crying with me. In the disco toilets, or sitting in a restaurant, I would have the entire table crying with me, including the waitron. I cried for my son, for the difficult path he had chosen, for the rejection he faced, for my grandchildren who would never be born. I cried for all the hopes and dreams I had for him. I understood why he had chosen this path: because of the deep rejection and abuse he had suffered at the hands of his father, the person whose love he wanted most.

Slowly, acceptance of who he was took the place of my disappointment and I started seeing my son through different eyes. I saw his true beauty and strength and acknowledged him for his courage to live his own truth. He was honest with himself. I had renewed respect for him.

RETURN TO SPIRITUALITY

DESPITE ALL MY SUCCESS AND material wealth I had achieved, I still felt a deep yearning to assist others with their healing. I instinctively knew that I had the ability to heal myself. I used to lay my hands on my body whenever I hurt myself and it would miraculously heal. It was not something I had ever thought about; it was a natural reaction. I would rub my hands together and, when they got hot and red, I would put them over the affected area and within minutes it would be completely healed. It was only as I grew up that I realised not everyone had this ability. In those days, I knew energy was at the heart of everything, but I had not been taught about it yet.

As a child, I devoured books on fairies, witches and space creatures, and was inexplicably drawn to mysticism and spirituality, which as I got older led me to read books on psychology and physiology. But spirituality and mysticism were what intrigued me the most.

Having grown up as a Christian and then converting to Islam I had felt that neither of those religions could satisfy my intense curiosity and my search for meaning. I studied paganism and witchcraft and learnt that witches were basically people who cared for the earth and plants. This led me to study herbalism and plant medicine in depth, and this in turn taught me that natural plant medicine is the only authentic medicine we need to heal our minds and bodies. I had renewed understanding and respect for our Mother Earth!

When I rented a three-bedroom apartment in Guangzhou, China, from where I ran my buying office, I also spent time in the Buddhist temples in my area, where I chanted with the monks and studied the life of Buddha. The temple was a ten-minute walk from my apartment and I would take my daily walk in silence or would join in the chanting with the monks. I loved the peaceful way of life and the respect they showed towards one another. They displayed very little aggression but huge tolerance, even though the place is crowded and over-populated. As much as the philosophy of Buddhism intrigued me, and I could relate to it somewhat, there was still something missing.

Insight:
I had a deep "knowing" that there was more to life than what I had been led to believe. I had experienced many unexplained miracles and mysteries in my life, which kept me wondering about other life forms. I instinctively knew I was born for a higher purpose, and that knowledge grew stronger every day!

My quest was to find my tribe, to belong, but somehow none of these religions or philosophies was a fit for me. Instinctively, I knew there was more, that my tribe was out there somewhere.

My search led me to study many healing modalities such as reiki, colour and pranic healing (energy healing),that presents a unique holistic approach used to treat a variety of ailments, from fever to heart conditions to cancer. By tapping into pranic or "ki" (chi) energy, we connect with the universal force that is our life force.

I qualified as a nutritionist, and as a psych-k practitioner, but I was insatiable. The more I learnt, the less I knew, as one lesson learnt exposed another. I was fascinated and intrigued by the power of the mind and was hungry for this kind of knowledge. I studied the works of professionals such as John Keheo, Wayne Dyer, Tony Robbins and Caroline Myss, and devoured all the books I could find on this topic. However, I was astounded to discover that Dr Bruce Lipton's book *Biology of Belief* was so in line with my personal beliefs about energy. I knew intuitively that our energy determines our physical health, and a healthy individual has a certain vibrational frequency.

As a child, I had applied healing energy with my hands to affected areas of my body, and it healed almost immediately, and I felt called to assist others in this way, but I was not ready to take the next step yet. My big dream was to build a healing retreat on an island, as I was a sun worshipper and believed the sun had healing powers. I had visited many islands in the Indian Ocean rim, but none of them seemed to have the right feel about them. They were all too commercial and touristy. I even flew my family on a private plane from Sydney, Australia, to view a private island that was for sale, but this too turned out to be wrong for me.

HOTEL CHAIN CONTRACTS

IN 2003, THREE YEARS AFTER my mother's passing, my father Graham moved in to live with me when I moved back to Constantia. He stayed with Sammy and Harry while I travelled to several African countries to procure hospitality contracts from big hotel chains such as the Serena Group and other independent hotels. I was offering a custom fabric-designing service, where I would design a fabric and colour to fit in with the theme and ambience of the hotel or corporation.

An on-line marketing exercise drew my attention to the Serena Group, founded by the Aga Khan fund, and we worked closely with their interior designers and buyers to refurbish some game lodges in the Serengeti. One of these projects included the seventy-roomed Mara Serena, which needed a revamp. Each chalet enjoyed expansive views over the African Savannah, stretching down to the banks of the Mara River. The lodge's exclusive position offered tourists the unique opportunity to watch the dramatic wildebeest migration, and the fabrics used had to be an exotic reflection of the wild life and untamed beauty.

I landed another contract with a four-star hotel in Mombasa, Kenya, called the Severin, where I designed fabrics to match their African theme in various colours of blue for the 200-bedroom hotel. I stayed at the hotel while awaiting the container of the made-up goods to arrive and, because it was delayed, I had lots of time on my hands. One morning, after breakfast, I went to sit on a hill overlooking the sea and saw in the distance another island. After asking the owner about the far away island, he told me that it was a place called Zanzibar.

ZANZIBAR

Up until then, Zanzibar had been just another mythical place like Timbuktu, and I was intrigued. I needed to visit this mystical place which was calling me and drawing me towards it.

The following day, I boarded a flight and spent a few days on the island of Zanzibar, where I immediately fell in love with the place. It resonated with me. It spoke to my soul and I instinctively knew that this was the island upon which I was going to build my healing retreat.

While staying at the beach in the South of Zanzibar, I ate fresh fish and explored the white sandy beaches and neighbouring villages, where I casually enquired if any land was available.

While working with the various hotels in Kenya, I decided to open a shop in Nairobi, where I employed Cat and her husband Luis to run the business. I rented a house, bought a vehicle and introduced Cat to the various hotels I with which I'd previously had contact. I sent a container filled with fabrics, sewing machines, curtain tracks and everything necessary to set up a self-sustaining curtain and upholstery retail shop.

Upon my return from Kenya, I received an email from one of the men who worked at the Zanzibar hotel I'd stayed at, telling me of the availability of some prime plots of land for sale in Zanzibar at a good price. Two weeks later I returned to the island, excited at the prospect of finding the perfect piece of paradise to build my healing retreat.

My search led to the Ministry of Land, where I met with Alie and Mr Shlenge, two employees who showed me many plots around the island. Then I finally found the perfect site on Pongwe

Beach, on the north-eastern part of the island. It was a private bay belonging to five different owners. Alie promised to track down the owners, who were living abroad, and to make them an offer for the land. I happily returned back to South Africa to raise the money for the property by starting to liquidate some more of my assets.

EXPANSION

I HAD ORIGINALLY HIRED AMINA to run the Furntex company and, because I'd found her to be very efficient, I promoted her to run the entire business when I wasn't around, which happened more often as I explored new markets in Africa. Amina was not only my assistant, but we became closer than sisters. I trusted her with my life. She often travelled with me to America, Europe and other countries when I was exhibiting my fabrics. With Amina in charge, I felt assured that my business was finally in good hands when I travelled abroad.

My trips as part of the delegation organised by the Chamber of Commerce took me to countries such as Nigeria, Angola, Ghana and East Africa. On one of these trips, I met a man called Alan who owned a security company that worked with most of the African governments and he was personal friends with most of the ambassadors and presidents. He invited me to the opening of the Equatorial Guinea's embassy in Pretoria. Despite their reported atrocious human rights abuses, South Africa now enjoyed full diplomatic relations with the Republic of Equatorial Guinea.

The then current president of eighteen years, Teodora Obiang Nguema Mbasogo, had, like his predecessor, called himself a god and created titles like "gentleman of the great islands of Bioko, Annobon and Rio Muni" and "El Jefe", which simply means the boss. His country had a reputation for being a "shabby tyranny", decayed by neglect and steeped in corruption.

In the early 1990s the fortunes of this tiny nation, with a population of no more than 1.2million, wedged between Cameroon and Gabon in West Africa, experienced a meteoric windfall. Mobil Corporation found oil offshore in 1996 and started pumping 80 000 barrels a day, ending Equatorial Guinea's downward financial trajectory and signalling their climb out of poverty. Although slightly delusional, the president used this opportunity to change the image of his country from rigged elections and a life expectancy of forty-eight years to a first world democracy. With one billion dollars in hand, he approached the South African government to rebuild his nation.

Alan, the boss of security, was in charge of bringing together big business, including Eskom, Murray and Roberts Construction and Southern Sun Hotels. He specifically identified contractors and consulting companies that would be able to help, and I, being the only woman amongst the delegation, was selected to complete the hotels and houses with interior decor.

I was given a brief by Alan that there were nine palaces to be completely refurbished and decorated, which was on top of the many hotels and houses that were to be constructed over a five-year period. My pitch focussed on projects ranging from the Miss World Pageant, supplying fabric to the dignitaries in Dubai, to having decorated five-star hotels in Africa.

I was introduced as a specialist in the decoration of palaces at an official meeting, which took place at their newly-opened embassy in Pretoria. When the delegation heard that I had decorated palaces in the past, the entire delegation looked at me with surprise. As I sat down, the warmth of embarrassment rushed up my neck as I ignored the curious and mocking looks at my "white lie".

Gambling and renovations had taken a big toll on my cash flow, so I desperately needed this contract to restore my bank balance. I could barely afford the R22 000 for my seat on the privately chartered plane. We had agreed to meet at Lanseria airport, just outside of Johannesburg, and the excitement was palpable. I greeted the few of the men I had met at the meeting and introduced myself to the rest whom I hadn't met before.

After take-off and settling down, lunch was served. I then fell into a deep relaxed nap, knowing I was in the capable hands of two experienced retired ex-South African Airways pilots. I was awoken when we landed to refuel in Namibia, before landing at our destination at Malabo international airport, located at Punta Europe on Bioko Island, which was basically a tin-roofed shack. At that stage, it only had one international flight and their government was the main user. In the 60s, during the Nigerian Civil War, the airport had been used as a base for flights in and out of Biafra.

On our arrival, the consultants were split up between the nine palace residences. I shared the one residence with the crew from the plane and became friends with the only other female, who was the air hostess.

I still shudder as I remember sharing my breakfast with a huge, colourful iguana lizard that casually launched itself onto the table and headed straight for my plate. I jumped up in fear and left my breakfast, vowing never to eat alone or outside again, no matter how romantic the setting.

Wandering around, camera in hand, I noticed that the predominant architectural style could have been described as Spanish Old Style. For three days, the consultants assessed their surroundings and planned a strategy forward. I agreed to present with Southern Sun and Rabie on the planned hotels and the two thousand houses to be constructed.

On the day of our departure, the contingent arranged to meet at 2.30pm at the airport so that the plane could be refuelled timeously in the Namibian desert, which closed at 6.30pm, but a few consultants were late. We eventually departed at 4.30pm and the owner of the aircraft informed us that we would not make the fuelling station in Namibia, but instead would have to fly via Angola to refuel. Consequently, our scheduled arrival time in Johannesburg was delayed by two hours.

Buoyant with success stories of mammoth signed-up orders, we all piled onto the plane. We celebrated with drinks and gourmet snacks laid on by the owner of the plane. Everyone slowly settled into their seats and, one by one, we dozed off.

PLANE "CRASH"

SITTING AT THE BACK, IN the second last seat with the ice and water buckets full of bottles of drinks just behind me, allowed for some privacy and calmness, which I needed after the past few days, which had been frenetic with constant meetings and functions. I must have fallen into a deep sleep as I was abruptly woken by a sudden jolt, throwing me forward and causing me to bump my head hard against the back of the seat in front of me.

I opened my panic-stricken eyes to the sight of thick black smoke billowing into the cabin from behind the grey curtain separating the passengers from the cockpit. The water from the ice buckets washed all over the floor and I saw the owner, who was sitting behind me, rushing to the front of the plane and returning with a burning object in his hands, before plunging it into the ice bucket that made another huge splash soaking me completely.

The pilot announced that they had lost a battery, which would affect the air and the heating system, and then the oxygen masks were lowered. The ringing in my ears and my heart pounding made it difficult to understand or comprehend what the pilots were saying on the speakers, as all I knew was that I was going to die.

The plane swayed from side to side and my body jerked in response to the sharp descent as the plane lost altitude.

Suddenly, the plane became icy cold, and my feet went completely numb. The owner was frantically running back and forth with hot water to melt the ice piling up on the windscreen, making it impossible for the pilots to see.

It all seemed so surreal, as if I were watching a movie upfront.

I saw some of the men up in front crying hysterically, some on their knees praying. I couldn't cry. I was numb with horror and disbelief. Fear gripped my chest and my heart palpitations made it difficult to breathe as I started hyperventilating, shaking uncontrollably. I struggled to put my oxygen mask on with my shaky hands.

My life flashed by and the only thing that mattered in that moment was my children. If only I could see them, hug them and tell them how much I loved them. Suddenly, I felt a pair of loving arms embracing and comforting me, as I heard her saying, "You will be okay, Libbet". A feeling of deep peace descended on me as I relaxed and detached myself from the chaos and hysteria around me.

We crash landed in Gaborone. Most of the passengers were in shock, some crying and others talking incessantly. The first flight took us to Johannesburg at 6am, where we greeted one another and headed home, knowing our lives would never be the same again. I had a connecting flight to Cape Town, so I had to wait around two hours before my flight. I went to the ladies' washroom to get rid of the huge ball of tears lodged in my throat, which was threatening to spill over at any moment. My tears came freely, and I cried for a long time in the toilets after realising that I had been saved from a certain death.

At this point, I was still in a state of shock, not realising what I had just survived. Fresh tears rolled down my cheeks as I was overwhelmed with wonder and gratitude. After some time, I gathered enough strength to enter Cafe Dulce, the closest restaurant to the bathroom. I donned my sunglasses, unable to control the tears flowing down my cheeks. I sat down, ordered a coffee, and then I heard a familiar sound coming from the radio. It was not a commercial song, but my mother's favourite hymn, which she had requested to be sung at her funeral. In a flash, memories of my mother singing at the top of her voice came rushing back to me.

I knew without a shadow of a doubt that my mother was with me on the plane, and that I had not imagined it.

POST-TRAUMATIC STRESS DISORDER

THE EUPHORIA OF SURVIVAL TURNED into a state of depression and darkness a few days later. As I was getting out of bed one morning, I felt lameness in my legs. I fell back onto the bed, unable to stand up. I suffered countless anxiety attacks just by being in a supermarket or driving my car. Nightmares and insomnia became the norm, and I was unable to regain normality. The compulsion to shift into the unknown became an obsession and the thought of stepping over seemed like the next step. It felt as if I had already died in the accident.

Insight:
It was only with hindsight that I realised that Ulrica actually died on the plane, as I was no longer able to run a business and material wealth lost all meaning for me. It hadn't been the solution it had promised to be. I was only interested in doing things that gave me pleasure and joy.

My psychologist eventually referred me to a psychiatrist, who misdiagnosed me with bipolar disorder after a few sessions. I was prescribed lithium, which put me in a zombie-like state, but the paralysis persisted. In the end, I had my sister Felicia move into my house to watch over me. It was she who helped me to lie or sit outside by the pool in the sun, and my father who joined us there while we spent hours outside.

It was on one of these sunny days when I looked up into the sun and heard these words: "Go to Zanzibar".

I replied, "I cannot walk and I have no money".

Within an hour, Cat called from Nairobi to tell me she had an order for a customer who owned a hotel in Zanzibar, but she didn't have enough stock to fill the order. We only had 100 metres in the storeroom, but this was exactly what Cat needed. The airfreight for these two rolls was expensive and, after Felicia called the airline, we discovered that it would be cheaper if we took it ourselves and put the fabric as part of our luggage allowance. The following day we were on the plane to Zanzibar.

On our arrival in Zanzibar, we checked into one of the hotels I had lived in previously in Stone Town. I went straight to bed and slept nonstop for three days, exhausted and unable to walk unassisted.

As Felicia was getting ready on the fourth day, she said, "Liz, you need some sunlight. Why don't you go to the beach with me for a short while?" I reluctantly agreed and, with the assistance of a hotel employee, I was carried to the beach and placed on a beach chair. It was nice to be outdoors again with the sun caressing my face as I got lost in my inner world.

From afar, I heard the voice of a man asking, "Liz, where have you been? I haven't heard from you. I found the owners of the land you were interested in, and they all agreed to sell it to you." I looked up into the eyes of Alie, the land guy.

It took me a while to fully grasp what he was saying as the words slowly penetrated my dazed mind. The moment I understood the amazing news, excitement and exhilaration surged through my body and I stood up, forgetting completely about my paralysis as I hugged him and thanked him profusely for his efforts in securing the land.

Insight:
I had found meaning in my life again! Another Miracle which left me in a state of deep gratitude!

With great purpose I returned home and began liquidating some of my properties to buy the land in Zanzibar.

Sadly, I discovered that in my absence Amina had defrauded my company of a vast amount. She was busy building a house with the help of Rudi. She had carried a huge amount of stock out of my shop as well as my sewing machines and had claimed my existing customers. After I confronted her, she left with all my employees and opened her own store. She had forged my signature on my company cheques. Absa Bank promptly refunded the money after I reported the matter to them, and they in turn sued Amina.

DEATH OF MY DAD

My dad still lived with us and often would enjoy the sunroom at the pool. I would often sit and drink my morning cup of tea with him before I went to work.

One morning, when I woke up to join my father in the sunroom where he spent most of his days, I noticed a bird sitting above the sun bed where my father sat. The bird sat in the same place every day, and no one could figure out what it was doing, as it wasn't flying around, eating or shitting.

I love birds. It was the one thing I remembered fondly as I was growing up. Every time I was stressed or sad, I noticed that birds would appear, openly staring at me as if to say, "I'm here for you". I always felt comforted by them.

As a child, I used to watch and assist Leo catch and "home" pigeons. This was exciting to watch, and I would assist with the process.

Birds always have special meaning for me, showing up at my lowest moments to comfort me.

I knew that birds were messengers from God, but this bird confused me, as I didn't know what it was saying. After the bird had sat there for two weeks, my father, who was suffering from angina heart disease, suddenly passed away from a heart attack in his bedroom. I thought he was sleeping in on the Sunday morning but later started being concerned, as my father was an early riser. I went into the bedroom to wake him up, but he felt cold. Hysterically I called Harry, who called 911. They arrived promptly and tried resuscitating him.

Meanwhile, another bird had joined the one which had sat there for two weeks. They just sat there inside the house, not moving, just staring. The medics tried for several hours but gave up and eventually announced Graham dead. As they were carrying Graham's covered body out of the house, a third bird flew into the window and joined the other two. It was the strangest thing we had ever seen as we observed how the three birds eventually flew out together, never to return. I believed the three birds were Maria, Bradley and Graham.

Healing Retreat

After my dad's funeral, I returned to focus on the Zanzibar project. I raised the money and purchased all five plots, totalling eight hectares (80 000 metres) of private bay. Zanzibar Health and Leisure Resort was registered in 2005. In order to get the project into Zipa's offices within a reasonable time, I had to bribe a number of people. It seems this is the norm when doing business in Africa. It was necessary to hire local professionals to do all the preliminary work, such as engineering plans, environmental impact studies, topographical reports and other studies that Zipa requested

The day I received Zipa's approval, and the building permit was issued, my team and I celebrated on my beach under the coconut trees, joined by the village chief and some of the villagers. The sun beckoned to me as if to bestow its blessing on me. Intuitively, I knew this was a gift! My piece of paradise!

I hired a guy I used to work with in Cape Town named Chris, who was older, very charismatic and an excellent artist, who painted the entire concept which was then given to a local architect to draw up.

Because there was no infrastructure on the plot, they couldn't start building until they had constructed underground water tanks, and water had to be delivered every day to fill these wells. The nearest municipality was six kilometres away and bringing water and electricity from the municipality was a long and expensive process. Subsequently, a wall was built with the foundation exceeding one metre below ground level.

My attempt at getting a loan from a South African bank was rejected, resulting in me having to liquidate even more assets. I eventually sold all my properties except the building in Retreat that was the Curtain Warehouse head office and still housed the only trading store. This building was in the process of being subdivided into ten factories, which I considered my pension fund should anything go wrong with the project.

I packed up most of my stock of furniture, fabrics, lighting, fabric and other merchandise I had been storing after closing all my shops except one and shipped it to Zanzibar. Chris had meanwhile managed to build a storeroom where all these goods were stored, to be used once the buildings were completed.

When I had raised enough money to build the first phase of the development, which consisted of twelve two-bedroom villas, the 600-metre swimming pool and 1000-metre restaurant/ conference centre, I then decided to set up an office in Guangzhou, China, to ship all the materials to Zanzibar, as I got a three-year tax exemption from the Zanzibar government.

Slowly, the first two-bedroom villa was completed. The large wooden French doors opening onto the terrace allowed for easy access to the beach, which was ten metres from the small garden in front. The terracotta stone cladding on the pillars was the perfect finish to complement the red cement floors and wooden windows. But for a few amendments, I was satisfied with the result. My excitement at seeing my creation come to life knew no bounds!

The next three villas on the beach front went up simultaneously, when the contractors employed more of the villagers. It was an impressive sight and when a few local property agencies and hospitality companies saw my project they immediately saw an opportunity for them to benefit, thus drawing my attention to how much money I could make if I sold the houses individually. Suddenly, the idea of a health retreat became a money-making resort. Greed had once again taken control, and I was lost in the material world once more.

I ran out of money and, while I was trying to raise additional funds on my properties, Chris left me to go and live and work in Dar es Salaam. I hired a foreman named Amani, who lived on site and liaised with the contractors. I found him honest and loyal, and we got along well.

In the meantime, I was looking for a person whom I could employ to manage the affairs on my site, who was reliable and trustworthy. I contacted Des, a friend who had expressed interest in relocating to Zanzibar with her husband Ron. Since Des and her husband are both re-born Christians, I felt I could trust them to handle my affairs in an honest and ethical manner.

There had been good progress in construction on Zanzibar, with the fourth beach front housing being constructed. I spent six months travelling around China, visiting the various markets, to find some of the most beautiful finishing materials, such as marble vanities, brass taps and silver cutlery. I waited in anticipation for the containers to arrive in Zanzibar so I could personally supervise the unpacking and storage of these valuables.

The main buildings had been constructed, but without doors and windows, so they used this facility for storage and barricaded them with wood and metal sheets. Once it was all safely stored, I left for Cape Town feeling reassured knowing that Des and Ron were on hand to supervise the completion of the structures. That very night after my departure from Zanzibar, the site was burgled and all the goods that had arrived from China were stolen. After the phone call from Des, informing me about the tragedy, I was in a state of shock as hopelessness and exhaustion overwhelmed me. I felt unable to function.

By 5am the following morning, I was back at the airport, exhausted and visibly agitated, my lack of sleep adding to my anxiety. My dear friend Salim, who met me at the airport upon my arrival, immediately took me to the local police station to report the matter. Several days later, some of the perpetrators were caught and imprisoned, but I did not receive my goods back.

After hiring a few investigators, I was able to track most of the goods to a rural farm near my site, where they were being stored and sold to the villagers. When I went to lay claim to all my goods, the local police kept them in their storeroom. However, when I returned to Cape Town, they returned all the goods to the guy who was selling them, claiming that he had bought them legally from the burglars. In the end, I lost the case and my products were seen in every household in the villages near my site.

My suspicion is that the police were conspiring with the individual who bought my goods. My rights were worthless in this foreign country, where men are superior and women are subordinate, and where money trumps justice.

This was a major setback for me because most of the money I had raised had gone to the purchase of those items and I had no idea how I could raise more money. The fastest way I could raise more money from my Retreat property, which was almost fully paid for, was to trust Rudi to buy it from me for half the value, so I could take the money to Zanzibar to complete the existing structures so that I could start trading. He assured me that he would sell the property to me for the same amount when I had the money to buy it back. He promised that he would put the property in a trust to protect my final valuable asset.

Not only was this project costing me financially, but I also became physically and emotionally exhausted due to the constant travelling between countries. My daughter also suffered, as I was an absent parent both physically and emotionally.

I became depressed by the continuous bad reports coming from site. With more than eighty people working on the site, there were continuous fights, tardiness and stealing. The money was running out fast and once again I had to put the development on hold as I could no longer afford to pay the contractors.

My dream had turned into a nightmare that was threatening to destroy me. My mind was paralysed by the magnitude of the challenges I faced. My tears were constantly threatening to overflow. It felt as if I was carrying the world on my shoulders.

As my mental health deteriorated, I became addicted to drugs to treat my insomnia and anxiety.

Then some relief came when I managed to secure a small loan from one of the local banks in Dar es Salaam and with this money I once again bought the last stuff I needed to complete the four villas so that I could start trading. I personally supervised the unpacking and storage of the containers when they arrived in Zanzibar. The storerooms were packed full again, and Ronny and Amani were supervising the construction of the buildings on site.

When the four villas were completed and the furniture and fittings installed, it was ready to be occupied, except that the pool and public areas still needed work. I gave Des the last $46 000 to complete the swimming pool, but shortly after she returned to Cape Town because she had personal issues to resolve, leaving Ron and Amani in charge of the site. After taking over the reins and liaising with the contractors, Ron made me believe that he was completing the pool and paying the contractors' salaries from the money I had left with them. As the pool was nearing completion, I was happy with the photos he sent me.

In my efforts to earn income from the resort, I tried everything from timeshare initiatives to outright sales, but without success. Every morning I woke up with a dark cloud hanging over my head, and I got super creative in trying to raise money to complete the project, but without success.

In 2008, I sold my curtain business to my brother for a pittance to raise money, as I no longer had an interest in the company and needed every penny for the resort. In an effort to accumulate enough money to complete the resort, I sold all my investment shares and everything else I could lay my hands on.

GROUPON

I GOT A BEE IN my bonnet about using the discounting website Groupon. We had a set of pictures of the villas, the pool and the beautifully landscaped gardens, terraces and fully-equipped bedrooms. It was possible for me to presell eight rooms for R5 000 per week for six months, which amounted to almost R1-million. In order to complete the villas, I had to purchase outdoor furniture. I requested an advance from Groupon, who gave me a 10% deposit. After the goods arrived and were cleared, Ron placed all the furniture where it was needed, and the resort was ready for guests. Or so I thought.

As a result of how well Ron was doing during my absence, I decided to extend my stay in Cape Town for another three months since Sammy was still enrolled at Reddam School and I wanted to be present for her as much as possible. My first guests were due to arrive the following week, so I decided to fly to Zanzibar two days before their arrival, but I only notified Ron a day before I left Cape Town. I left with excitement and anticipation - I couldn't wait to see the progress on my resort - but when I arrived on site my heart sank. The site looked the same as it had three months before and Ron was nowhere to be found.

The original goods transported from South Africa, that had been carefully placed in the rooms were missing. All the goods, including expensive fabrics, lighting and furniture, which had been stored on site, were gone. This included the new items that I had bought with the deposit from Groupon. The pool was raw concrete and the gardens were simply dunes.

Ron had allegedly had sexual orgies with young girls and had gambled all the money I had given him and Des. As a result, he'd accumulated gambling debt, so he'd had to sell my remaining goods to pay his debts. The site was desolate. It looked like a ghost town, with no one living there, and the water and electricity had been disconnected; it looked like a ghost town.

I was horrified. My guests had already arrived on the island, and those who had reached my resort first found it to be a deserted building site. A tourists' worst nightmare. For the first time in my life, I had nowhere to hide and no one to turn to. I had no money to pay for a hotel and I couldn't go back to the site for fear of the guests arriving and finding me there.

As I entered a popular hotel, I saw my photo stuck on their board at reception, with the words "Wanted". I left very quickly, hiding under my sunhat and dark sunglasses. It transpired that Groupon had contacted the Zanzibar authorities and I was now a wanted person on the island, which meant I couldn't leave as they would be waiting for me at both the airport and seaport.

I went to sit in a bar, in a dark corner, hoping to track Duncan, a friend I'd met previously in Stone Town, down, hoping he could assist me. In a state of panic, I tried to make myself invisible, feeling like a fugitive on the run, too afraid to show my face or go to the popular cafes and restaurants I used to frequent. This was the end of the line, and I didn't know how I could escape this situation. I was completely homeless. I couldn't even message anyone or go to an internet café to contact my family and friends.

Eventually, Duncan entered the bar after I had spent several hours hidden in my corner and I burst into tears at the sight of him. Filled with sympathy and compassion, he looked at me. He had heard the bad news, which had spread like wildfire all over the island. A fraud case had been filed against me by Groupon in South Africa and in Zanzibar.

Duncan immediately contacted them and managed to smooth things over temporarily while making alternate accommodation arrangements for the existing guests now stranded on the island. Groupon had managed to stop most of the guests but couldn't stop those who were already on their way.

In the end, I had no choice but to return to my site and stay in the first villa, which at least had a mattress where Ron had slept after he had sold everything. In the absence of electricity, I had no choice but to sleep as soon as darkness fell, which meant I had to sleep with open windows because of the oppressive heat and humidity. The mosquitoes feasted on me, and I became purple and swollen on my arms, legs and face.

I was forced to drink dirty water from one of the underground tanks that the workers used to rinse themselves to quench my thirst and to clean off my sweat and grime. The water, which was also used for building purposes, became my fountain of life. I managed to gather enough dry wood to make a fire, which enabled me to sterilise the water. I found some tea bags and was grateful for those small mercies. The bananas I bought from a hawker on credit got me through the day. My days were very dark, and I seriously considered running into the sea.

THE PRAYER

I WAS FURIOUS WITH GOD. "How could You do this to me? Why?" I demanded as I sobbed hysterically.

After my tirade at God, I was no longer able to fight. I collapsed onto the grey cement floor in hopelessness and resignation, with nothing left to fight for. I could just lie there and die. Just then, a flock of birds flew into my open window and sat on my cupboard, all staring at me. I intuitively understood their presence meant that they wanted to comfort me and tell me that everything would be okay.

The following day, Lamway, an ex-employee, came to the site looking for me. He had learned of my arrival from the villagers and came to request his wages, since the contractors had not paid him for two months. Ten minutes later, a mob of thirty-six men arrived, armed with pangas and axes. They were chanting and swearing in Swahili, which I didn't understand, but I instinctively knew from their tone that they were angry and dangerous. They didn't speak or understand English, so Lamway translated on their behalf. The men demanded payment for the work they had done, but I explained to them that Ron had paid the contractors that employed them.

There was no interest in explanations as mass hysteria gripped them. One youth lifted his panga and threatened to attack me, while the others cheered him on. My body was frozen to the spot, and I couldn't move or utter a word but silently prayed. At this point, Lamway dropped to the ground and started praying in Swahili. Suddenly, the mob stopped their chanting and joined him in prayer.

I sat as tears of relief and gratitude streamed down my face as I grasped the miracle that had just happened. On completing their prayers, I promised to return and pay all the workers as soon as I could. As a result of Duncan's assistance, Groupon retracted their charges, and I was allowed to leave the island and return home. I said goodbye to my dream, knowing in my heart that I would never return to this piece of land that had been given to me by God. This dream had turned into a nightmare, but it came with a lifetime of lessons learned! It had taken up ten long years of my life.

Insight:
With hindsight, I realised how everything fell apart when my intention changed. My initial motivation was to build the retreat for the greater good of humanity and mid-way I became greedy as I started seeing the monetary value of the project!

RUDI LIQUIDATED

I RETURNED TO CAPE TOWN and walked off the plane and into another storm. Rudi, who had started a diesel company the previous year, had bought R16-million worth of diesel trucks, but when the company ran into trouble, Mercedes had no option but to repossess the trucks. Luckily, Rudi assured me that my building and house were safely parked in a trust. My only income was now from the eleven factories I was still renting, but that money was going towards paying the small loan I had taken out for Zanzibar. Rudi was in arrears with Absa, who decided to legally sue him in court. The case dragged on indefinitely. I discovered to my horror that he had never transferred my building or my house into a safe trust, but instead had used my property as surety against the loan for the diesel trucks.

While the court case was dragging on, I was living with my teenage daughter in our big house. Since I had no income and could not maintain the pool or garden services, I'd had to let my maid go. Because I'd sold my car in order to send money to Zanzibar, I could not drive Sammy to her school in Westlake and had to ask some of the parents to lift her. Her school fees were in arrears and the threat of expulsion hung over her head. It was embarrassing for both of us. Our only source of food was a R5 packet of Marie biscuits and peanut butter.

Tommy, one of my closest friends, sometimes brought food over, for which I was extremely grateful, but I still felt embarrassed to accept her charity since I was not a graceful receiver. This made me feel like a failure, a beggar, and less than. I was the one who used to give, not receive. I had too much pride.

Insight:
I could then identify how small I must have made others feel with my constant help and charity. Giving gave me a sense of power, which reduced the receiver to an unspoken debt of obligation, which resulted in them feeling resentment and probably hatred towards me.

SOLLY AND MART

WHEN SOLLY FINALLY CAME OUT about being gay, he moved into one of my apartments in Green Point while he was attending UCT. As Solly formed new relationships with the gay community, one of those friends introduced him to drugs. In the beginning, I was unaware of his addiction. It wasn't until after my mother's death that I saw for myself how serious his addiction had become. I intervened by forcing him to leave these places where the drugs were freely available, sometimes chasing him around the flats where he was "high". I felt helpless and utterly powerless. My heart broke when I saw what was happening to my son, the child I had tried to protect with my life.

In the same way that I suffered from an addiction, his addiction was a way to avoid facing his pain and trauma. I decided to use "tough love" and threw him out of my house and he moved in with his father. With the help of his grandmother, who supported me in my quest, we confiscated his car, his mobile phone and his pocket money. He hated me, but this was my last resort to save my son.

He eventually got off the drugs and completed his degree and honours at university, where he met his boyfriend Mart. He became a successful model and thereafter joined his father in selling furniture and curtains in Paarden Eiland.

Solly and Mart shared one of the two cottages outside the main house. Solly and Harry were working with their father, selling furniture and fabrics from the Paarden Eiland shop. When the Paarden Eiland shop was seized by the liquidators, Solly and his partner moved out to a small flat just outside of the Constantia

Village, where he tried to run a small showroom from his lounge. He eventually built his business into a very successful and well-known fabric company in Constantia. He is still with his partner Mart and seems stable and happy in his life.

HARRY

HARRY IN MANY WAYS RESEMBLES his father, and they share a very special bond. Harry is quiet and aloof but quite intimidating, with a seething anger just beneath the surface - and anything can set it off. He constantly accused me of loving his older brother Solly more than him. Harry probably felt this way because I've always protected Solly since he was a small, timid boy, and Harry was a much more confident and stronger child, or so it appeared to me. I felt guilty about this, so I always tried to make him feel special. He was also very angry at this father's betrayal by having another son during our marriage and eventually marrying the mother. I tried my hardest to make him happy but his anger and my guilt stood in the way of our relationship. When Harry turned twenty-one, we threw a big party where he met Melanie, who is now his wife. He fell head over heels in love with her and they moved into the second flat on the property.

SISTER AVA

MY YOUNGEST SISTER AVA, WHO lived in Australia and Johannesburg for a few years, moved back to Cape Town with her children, Kelly and Tres, to live with Sammy and me. At the time, Cat was also living with us. However, none of us had an income at all and we had three small children to feed. Cat managed to make a few Rand by sewing and selling scatter cushions.

Ava studied Sports Therapy Massage in Queensland and has become highly skilled in her field. By advertising her services in local newspapers, she managed to secure a client willing to pay R600 for a stress relief massage. Melanie had just purchased my massage bed from me and had promised to pay me when she had the money. I sent the girls over to her flat to ask her if we could borrow the bed for two hours, but she said she had already sold it to a friend. Sammy and Kelly, however, told me they'd seen a bed in the corner of their bedroom, and when I confronted her, she admitted it was still there.

She reluctantly gave me the bed but called Harry to tell him what had happened. Harry arrived in the driveway a few minutes later and, as his car came to a grinding halt in front of his cottage, he jumped out and fetched his cricket bat. Sarah, our domestic, saw what was happening and ran inside to warn us. We anxiously scattered in different directions to hide from Harry's fierce temper.

Harry was determined to break into the house to attack me with the bat, and he hurled threats at me through the locked door. As I trembled in fear, my head spun in shock at the realisation that my son wanted to harm me. My anxiety reached new heights and I struggled to breathe. I called the cops, who responded a short while later, but Harry had already left and moved out. After filing an assault charge, the sheriff visited me with a court date for the Wynberg courtroom a few weeks later.

As the court date drew closer, I was filled with dread. The day finally came when I had to face Harry in court. I was visibly nervous when I arrived at court and almost tripped on the steps. I caught a glimpse of Harry, as his father escorted him into the courtroom. The fact that his father was also there unnerved me even more and, when I was asked to relate my part of the story, I was tongue tied. Words failed me as I tried fighting back the tears that were threatening to spill over. At the time, the incident was still so fresh, and I hadn't even begun dealing with the pain. I sat speechless as tears flowed down my cheeks and down my neck. Loud sobs escaped my throat as I listened to these two big men describing me as crazy.

According to my ex-husband, I had made his life miserable and now I was falsely accusing his son of something he would never even consider. He suggested I should be institutionalised. His words were like a dagger stabbing into my heart as these two people I'd once loved tore me apart. The magistrate seemed sympathetic towards them and encouraged me to seek counselling.

I walked out of the courtroom as the tears continued to flow down my cheeks, not caring about the looks of sympathy that I glimpsed on some of the faces of the people sitting on the benches lining the corridors.

My heart was broken into a million pieces.

Nothing mattered except the betrayal and intense pain inflicted by the son I had laid down my life for! It was undeniably one of the saddest times of my life, when my son publicly rejected and condemned me.

On the way home, my emotions fluctuated between deep despair and rage, and I wanted nothing more than to seek revenge on Rudi. I cursed him with an intensity, as pure hatred consumed my entire being. I wanted him to hurt the way I was hurting.

Insight:
Now that I know that I actually cursed myself, I take responsibility for my loss. Consequently, what I wished would happen to him, happened to me, and I lost everything I had worked for.

A few years later, I reconciled with Harry when Melanie gave birth to a little girl named Madi, with whom I immediately fell in love. There was no mention of the incident and Harry never apologised to me. I tried to pretend I wasn't hurting any longer, but the pain was still there, lying dormant. This caused a rift in our relationship but, as usual, I buried the pain inside and avoided dealing with it.

PROTECTED

I WAS DAZED AND DISORIENTATED from all the drugs I was taking to function: one to sleep and one to wake up, and then some sedatives during the day to keep me from falling apart.

Sometimes, I was not even sure what day of the week it was. It was on one of these blurry days that a friend of Solly, a very spiritual young man who had converted to Islam, came to knock on the door, telling me he had been sent by Sai Baba*, the Indian saint whom I had discovered through my spiritual search. In fact, I had made a pilgrimage to Bangalore, his home city in India, to meet with him, but he was on a tour and has since passed away.

It seems he had known about me all along and had telepathically conveyed a message to this young man to bring some of his mysterious Vibuti (holy ash) to comfort me during this very dark and painful time in my life. The small package with this ash was wrapped in a piece of white paper with a prayer written on it. I was amazed at the mystery of this incident as I had never met the man personally and only ever worshipped at his temple occasionally. I found great comfort in this precious gift and carried it with me wherever I went.

Looking out over the expanse of the garden to the trees one morning, I noticed an unusual phenomenon. In the bright daylight sat an owl, looking directly at me. I had never seen the owl before, but I sometimes heard him at night. Now, he sat staring at me with his big eyes from the tree where he was sitting. The owl sat there the entire day and many days after. He then moved to sit on the chair at the poolside, sitting there day and night, watching over me as if guarding the house. Then he moved to perch on my terrace chair. This phenomenon went on

---

*   Sathya Sai Baba; 23 November 1926 – 24 April 2011) was an Indian guru and philanthropist. At the age of fourteen, he claimed that he was the reincarnation of Shirdi Sai Baba] and left his home in order to serve the society and be an example to his followers.

for more than a week. At first, I became alarmed thinking the owl brought bad news but I knew instinctively that it came to be with me in those dark days. He brought such comfort and I felt loved and protected.

LIQUIDATION

RUDI LOST THE CASE AGAINST Absa and the liquidators had taken over the estate, which included my eleven factories and my house. A few days after the court verdict, there was a knock on the door and the auctioneers came in to inspect the house before fixing their auction boards outside the property. The public auction never occurred as they had privately sold my building and house for a fraction of the value, and I was given days to vacate the property. At this stage, the only valuables I had left were a few pieces of furniture and my clothes. I had sunk into a deep depression, not sure whether I was coming or going, my emotions veering between self-pity to helplessness to hopelessness!

The dreaded day finally arrived when the liquidators came and changed my locks, giving us six hours to move all my belongings out of the house. Solly and Harry arrived with a truck and a few men, who helped carry as many of our belongings out of my four-bedroom house as they could. My clothes and personal belongings were packed in boxes and those were stored in Mart's garage where he was now living with Solly in Lakeside. At the end of that day, I had to leave quite a few valuables behind, including a very expensive fabric measuring machine that was later destroyed or sold off, as I wasn't allowed to go back to collect it.

DARKEST DAY

Waking up in Mart's garage the next day was probably one of the saddest days of my life. In deep despair, I looked over the few boxes of clothing, paintings, and precious books I had managed to salvage from the liquidators. Thirty years of hard work stored in a few boxes was too much to bear and I cried, unrestrained sobs wracking my body until exhaustion took over and I slept and sobbed some more. There was no point in getting out of bed. What for?

Not only had I lost my physical belongings, but I had also lost my power, my confidence. My self-esteem and self-worth were at an all-time low. Money had given me a false sense of power, which had made me feel invincible! Without the money, what was I?

As Rudi one day commented in Solly's shop, "You are a 'fuck-all' and you have 'fuck-all'!" This comment brought me back to my childhood, when I had been made to feel like a "dirty rag", but this time I didn't feel anger; instead only a deep sadness. I had come full circle and was back to where I had started, not realising how much I had actually grown.

I struggled to find my attributes; my strength and courage seemed to have died with me in that plane. I was looking at myself through the lens of "failure" and came up with useless, no education, no skill, only shame being my constant companion.

"How can I even start over again as I have nothing?" I reminded myself over and over again.

Insight:

My success did not give me the love and approval I had so yearned for. Instead, I was more alone now than I had ever been! My money was an extension of myself; it was a reward for the energy I had exerted. But, since I didn't value myself, I didn't value my money either.

Losing my money was, in hindsight, the best thing that could have happened to me. I finally found my beauty and my purpose when I had nothing to offer but my unique gifts!

BLEAK FUTURE AHEAD

THE FUTURE LOOMED DARK AHEAD of me and picking myself up seemed almost impossible. I was exhausted and did not have the energy to lift myself out of my depression. Instead, I was wallowing in self-pity. "How do I start picking up the pieces? What can I do?" I had nothing to start over with, and these were the questions that plagued me every minute of every day. I felt helpless, despondent, and did not see any opportunities. I felt like a cat that had used up its ninth life.

I spent every day beating myself up, the cycle of regret, guilt and shame perpetually replaying itself, until slowly the realisation dawned on me that I had become greedy with the Zanzibar project, which was supposed to have been a healing retreat instead of a money-making resort.

I was in this dark, negative space of self-pity and self-blame and felt helpless to lift myself out of it.

As I stood in the kitchen one evening, I suddenly felt a rush of blood from my vagina. I knew it wasn't normal as I'd been post-menopausal for the past four years. I knew something serious was wrong and immediately rushed to the pharmacy. The pharmacist advised me to urgently get medical treatment at an emergency room.

Without medical insurance or money to attend a private hospital, I waited for hours in line at Groote Schuur for the doctor who, following an intense examination, found two huge fibroids in my uterus that were diagnosed as malignant. He scheduled an operation, but I had to go on a six-month waiting list.

The diagnosis forced me to confront my negative state of mind and made me realise just how precious life was and how many things I still wanted to accomplish. Knowing that I had caused my illness, I knew that I was the only one who could heal it. The condition of my mind determined my emotions and physical state, and I knew exactly what I had to do to heal.

I made a mental shift from self-pity to gratitude, changed my eating habits, and with this new positive attitude I healed my body. A visit to the hospital a month later confirmed the tumours had shrunk and that they were benign. There was no need for a hysterectomy. They never completely disappeared, but I see them as a blessing in disguise because, whenever I consume too much sugar or junk food, the tumours play up, reminding me that I am on the path to self-destruction.

Insight:

I realised that disease and sickness are not our enemies, but that they are messages from our souls, telling us that we need to process and release pain and trauma or make the needed positive changes in our lives or the physical result is disease.

A GLIMMER OF HOPE

SINCE I HAD NO MONEY and no place to go to work, I stayed at Mart's house in Lakeside. I took advantage of the internet and studied a variety of self-improvement strategies. I enrolled myself in every free course and webinar of interest and detached from the problems of Zanzibar for a while.

When I had procured a loan from the bank in Tanzania, I made friends with two bank assistants who were very helpful and who had been in regular contact with me. They contacted me to tell me that the bank was about to auction my resort and that the auction was set to take place the following week. The bank had also been trying to sell the resort privately to some of their existing clients before the auction. Simultaneously, ZIPA was also in the process of taking legal action against my property, as I was in arrears of lease payment for more than five years.

I had expected this, but I was exhausted and past caring. I handed the matter over to God without fear of the outcome and carried on with the job of putting my life back together in Cape Town. A few days later, I received a call from one of the bank assistants, who explained that they had found an interested buyer for my resort and asked if I could come to Zanzibar to discuss the matter. I borrowed money from Solly, who at this stage was running a successful curtain business, and caught a flight to Zanzibar. When I met with the potential buyer, we negotiated a price that I was very happy with. In fact, I would have been ecstatic to walk away from the resort with half of the agreed price, just to have my peace of mind back. I was grateful that I was finally rid of this project without having suffered a heart attack or stroke, although my mental health had taken a serious knock.

After many months of legal documents passing from attorney to attorney, the buyer finally paid two-thirds of the agreed purchase price. However, I was beside myself with excitement and gratitude at the miracle that had once again taken place in my life. I'd learned invaluable life lessons from the Zanzibar project. I may have lost everything that I had worked for in monetary terms, but I gained so much more in personal growth.

Insight:
The trauma and pain I had experienced in a decade of being involved with the Zanzibar project stood me in good stead for the next chapter of my life. I viewed money as a bonus for living my passion and not the sole purpose of accumulation. Life had taken on a new meaning for me and that was to seize every moment and live it to the fullest!

AYAHUASCA

WITH ZANZIBAR BEHIND ME, A month before I set out to go on my long-awaited Italian adventure, to purchase my dream house on Lake Como, a promise I had made to myself twenty-six years earlier, Solly introduced me to a spiritual healer who was a shaman, who facilitated healing with a visionary plant called Ayahuasca*.

Having always been spontaneous, I agreed to take part in a healing ceremony with a few friends, which was scheduled to take place the following day at a friend's house. Upon our arrival, we were told to find our own space in the room and the Shaman gave us a vile tasting dose of his brew from the Ayahuasca plant.

The inner journey lasted almost six hours, where I relived several past lifetimes and with each lifetime came the continuation of lessons incomplete from the previous one.

Some of the insecurities and fear I was dealing with in this lifetime originated in one of the previous ones.

My commitment phobias, the unworthiness of love, fear of cats and so many other fears and insecurities that kept me stuck in my lonely box, originated way back in previous lifetimes. I asked God after every death, "Where were you?" The answer was always the same: "I was always there. I am in the darkness and the light! There cannot be light without there being darkness. We only grow from darkness and pain."

---

* Ayahuasca is a brew made from the Banisteriopsis caapi and Psychotria Viridis plants. Taking Ayahuasca leads to an altered level of consciousness due to psychoactive substances in the ingredients.

Coming out of this experience removed my blinkers and clarified so many unanswered questions I'd had about life and my purpose. I experienced a connection to everyone and everything and each one I met brought with them a gift. This experience opened up my vision and suddenly everything became clear to me. All the pain and trauma of my loved ones were part of the lessons I needed to learn to move forward towards my spiritual growth.

Insight:
I understood that all the people who'd hurt and betrayed me were my teachers who had come to teach me valuable lessons of self-acceptance, self-respect, self-worth and self-love. God told me that I should not be afraid to love, as love is who I am, and when I deny someone love, I deny myself love.

I realised that I needed to stop harbouring the resentment and bitterness that I felt for my family and Rudi, so I performed the selfish act of forgiving and releasing them, so that I could make space for love and joy in my life. I understood then what Karl and so many good men had seen in me, to which I was blinded. I had become very nonchalant about my surroundings. My values and my priorities had changed and I no longer valued material things as much as before. I'd amassed great wealth and had lost it. People and relationships took on greater importance and I knew that when I had wealth, I wasn't happy or at peace. Money and material wealth came with certain responsibilities that I no longer wanted to have. I had achieved everything and more I had ever dreamt of and was finally ready for my next adventure and spiritual journey.

COMO

I ARRIVED IN COMO IN April, on a rainy day full of anticipation and excitement at living in my own paradise! This was one of the many dreams on my bucket list that had yet to be achieved. I set out on my search with an estate agent, whom I had contacted before arriving in Italy, and the very first house she showed me was The One!

The three-storey ancient villa was situated in the centre of the lake had the most magnificent views of Lake Como. It was the very first property I viewed, and it was waiting for me, a rare find. The house was in disrepair and needed serious renovation, as everything was old, including the infrastructure. After getting a few quotes for the work to be completed to upgrade the house and bring it back to its noble splendour, I set off to find building material. I was recommended to a store in Como called OBI, one of the largest hardware chains in Europe.

I walked into the store with my long list of building supplies, but there was only one assistant who spoke broken English and -with great effort- he tried to assist me as much as he could. After a while, he called another salesman to relieve him. A short young man strode towards us. He wore a crisp white shirt and orange tie. Because of his attire and the way in which he approached us, he seemed to hold a superior position. He introduced himself as Luca, the manager of the store. Despite his limited English, he managed to help me out as much as possible and I purchased whatever was needed for the upgrade of the house.

LUCA

THE MOMENT I LOOKED INTO Luca's eyes, there was a sense of instant recognition. I felt like I knew him, but that was impossible as I had never met him in my life before. The feeling of familiarity was disconcerting, but I couldn't shake it off. I was convinced I'd known him in a previous lifetime. The attraction to Luca was strong and I wanted to get to know him better, but he looked young enough to be my son. I felt alarmed and embarrassed by my feelings and admonished myself for my madness. Luca was equally enamoured by me and offered me a 20% discount on all goods purchased from his shop.

Luca did not fit the mould of my type of man. In fact, he was quite the opposite of "tall, dark and handsome", being short, fair and balding. His beauty shone through. His obvious traits of honesty and sincerity screamed integrity. The bond between us was incredibly strong and, as much as I threatened many times to walk away, I couldn't bring myself to do so. Falling in love with a young man, seventeen years my junior, was never something I'd considered, certainly not after I saw how my sister Cat and my friend Jenny were both hurt and rejected by the young men they were involved with. During past love affairs, I was in complete control of my feelings and could walk away at the drop of a hat if things became too serious. My commitment phobia never allowed me to move up to the next level to have a serious relationship.

The Ayahuasca journey led me to face many of my deep-seated fears and phobias. Things suddenly started happening in fast forward - I would think or speak of something and it would happen. The synchronicities were far too frequent for it to be coincidental.

It was as if my growth had accelerated and I wanted to grow instead of continuing with my usual pattern of avoidance, but it was scary as it meant I had to make myself vulnerable and to trust. This was a very frightening place to be.

Within my relationship with Luca, I was confronted with one of my greatest fears. Falling in love with a much younger man was a whole new level of fear. But I knew in my wisdom that he came as a teacher to teach me about love. As God said in my journey, "Love is not conditional; it doesn't have a face or an age. Love just is!" I was consumed by my inner conflict of running or facing this fear. It exhausted me, but I was powerless. This attraction I felt towards this young man was stronger than me. It seemed that running from commitment had finally caught up with me.

LOVE AFFAIR

LUCA PERSISTED IN COURTING ME and I very badly wanted to transcend my fear of rejection and experience intimacy and love on a deeper level than I'd ever had with any other man. Once I accepted him as a serious partner, I started to appreciate the value he brought into my life. I admired his discipline and strong values that I subscribed to and knew that I could either hold onto my point of view or learn what he had to offer.

Luca was my exact opposite, liking everything I disliked or feared. I was suddenly faced with insecurities about my ageing body, unreasonable jealousy when we were in the company of younger, attractive women and the unfamiliar food and the language was a huge barrier. It just seemed to be the most incompatible and uncomfortable union and all I wanted to do was run. I realised that I had been running away from my pain all my life, as it was easier than facing it. It was time I stopped and looked at what was in front of my eyes. I knew deep in my soul that Luca came into my life as a teacher, if I was prepared to learn what he came to teach me.

A few months into the relationship, he subtly began criticising things about me: my underwear not matching, my unkempt nails, my clothes, the way I did things that, in his opinion, were not "good enough". I accepted his criticism as constructive and started buying sexier underwear and changed my style of dressing so I could look younger, making sure my nails and hair were always impeccable.

I desperately sought his approval.

Luca adored me and set out to make all my dreams come true, starting with taking me to see my favourite singer Bocelli at his estate in Tuscany. He treated me like a princess and when he asked me to marry him, I accepted without hesitation. I was ready to walk this path with him and for him to take me to the next level of my life's journey. This was the prince I'd been waiting for all my life! I knew in my soul that we were meant to be together and that, no matter what, he would be my soft landing, my coming home to, my partner, lover and friend.

Luca set out to arrange a wedding fit for a princess. Together with the help of his sister, he planned to have a small but intimate ceremony in a 100-year-old Castle on Lake Como.

It was to be everything I had dreamt my wedding should be: a fairy-tale!

THE WEDDING

ON THE MORNING OF THE wedding, I panicked and the idea to run became a very big temptation. There was excitement and quiet chaos in the house as Solly, Sammy, and three of my girlfriends from South Africa ran about the old house, trying to get ready, while I was dealing with my private drama: my wedding dress wouldn't fit. I had bought the dress online and had it made smaller when I was still in South Africa, but that was two months prior to the wedding, before friends and family had arrived and we had sampled too many Italian restaurants, eating pasta and other delicacies Much to my dismay, the zip of my wedding dress refused to close.

I was a nervous wreck. I prayed to God to let all this pass because I couldn't possibly face the guests, many of whom I didn't even know. The dress was so very tight I couldn't breathe or sit, I had no idea how I was going to make it through the day without being able to sit. My dream had suddenly turned into a nightmare and the idea of running away seemed to be the only way out of this disaster. I had all these doubts running through my mind. I was suddenly face-to-face with the reality that I was getting married - to a much younger man from a different culture.

When it all dawned on me, I wanted to cry and laugh hysterically at the same time. I asked myself, "What was I thinking?"

Jenny, my close friend and bridesmaid, saved the day. With her needlework experience, she managed to sew a piece of elastic into the waistline that gave me the breathing space to move around with ease. I could have kissed Jenny's feet, I was so relieved and grateful.

I looked like a princess in my white damask mermaid dress, fitted snugly to every curve of my tall, slender body, and a crown of white flowers in my hair. This was the day I had dreamt of and visualised all my life since I was a little girl. This was another dream coming true. I was a princess! I deserved all of this and more! Gratitude and love for my "Father" overflowed!

When it was time to leave the room and venture outside to meet the wedding car, I was trembling from nervousness and I almost stumbled on the pavement as I tried getting into the car with my tight mermaid dress and high heeled shoes. However, I felt comforted by Solly's strong grip on my arm.

Meanwhile, Luca was anxiously pacing the pavement outside the old Castello, fearing that I might have had second thoughts. Solly and I eventually got into the wedding car driven by Marco, Luca's brother-in-law, and set off to the venue, where Luca visibly breathed a big sigh of relief when we finally arrived. Luca looked dashing in his navy silk suit with a white crisp shirt and silver silk tie. He looked more handsome than I'd ever seen him look, and I was struck by how deeply I had fallen for him.

As we walked down the stairs, beautifully decorated with white roses and green manicured trees, to greet the guests who were animatedly snapping away with their cameras, I felt secure with my hand firmly in Luca's.

The ceremony was a blur for me, as it was performed in Italian then translated by a sworn translator. I was very relieved when it was finally time to sign the big book that meant we were now officially and legally married. We could enjoy the festivities that Luca and Sabi had so painstakingly arranged and planned for the past three months.

The guests all left to enjoy typical Italian delicacies and prosecco at the beautiful restaurant on the lake, while Luca and I sailed across to the small port town of Sala Comacina to pose for the wedding photographer. Later, the guests joined us at his sister's estate to enjoy course after course of gourmet Italian food, prepared by one of Como's finest chefs. It was one of the most magical days of my life, and we danced the night away to typical South African music. A wave of nostalgia hit me as I kissed and thanked all my loved ones who had made the long trip to attend my wedding.

I waved goodbye to everyone while we climbed the gangway of the huge passenger liner to begin our romantic Mediterranean cruise. It was a magical departure, with Bocelli singing in the background, the perfect send-off for our new life together.

HIS OCPD

I HAD DISCOVERED THAT LUCA was suffering from OCPD (obsessive-compulsive personality disorder) when I first visited his flat. I'd had to remove my shoes and put on house-slippers, which I readily accepted as his house rules. Then, when I stepped outside onto his tiny one-metre-wide terrace, I had to remove the house slippers to don the terrace slippers. There was something extremely frustrating about it.

The flat came with an unwritten manual of what and what not to do, which I learned by trial and error. The bathroom was extra special, as it had wooden floors and the one bathroom mat had to be moved around, according to wherever I was, to outside the shower, next to the basin, or the toilet, so as not to spill any water on the floor.

The rules drove me crazy, and I was extremely nervous and anxious in his company especially when I was in his flat. I seemed to do everything the wrong way or in the wrong order. It felt like I was treading on eggshells. I was freaked out as I had become very nonchalant about my surroundings since my plane incident, not taking things so seriously and simply being grateful for just being alive and healthy. My values and priorities had changed, and I no longer valued material things as much. So, the OCPD took some getting used to.

In the beginning, every comment or criticism affected me, though. I felt inadequate, old and ugly. I found myself constantly apologising for some mistake I had made or something I had overlooked.

I noticed every stretch mark on my body. Every wrinkle and mark on my face would torment me until I could cover it with make-up. He constantly found another and yet another mistake and I believed he was teaching me to do things "properly, more efficiently, to be better than who I was," but sadly I could never seem to please him. Because I was so nervous and tense when he was around, I made stupid mistakes, which made me feel even more inadequate. I tried to spend as little time as possible in his presence so I could breathe and relax.

The relationship was tumultuous from the beginning. The ups and downs were destructive and addictive at the same time. My feelings for him ranged from intense dislike, bordering on hate, and then intense love. The bond I felt was very confusing, yet I couldn't get myself to leave the relationship. It was as if a strong force was keeping me there and I was determined to give this marriage my all.

All I'd ever wanted was my mother's approval and love. I'd then attempted to access these feelings through Rudi and more latterly Luca. Gradually, I started to care less about what he thought I should wear or how I should look. I began to enjoy the little things that gave me pleasure without having to constantly be on the alert. I started to enjoy being me, with my unstructured lifestyle, my love for chocolates, my bubbly personality, and carefree spirit, but mostly my rebellious nature and disregard for rules, which earned me the reputation of "being wild", according to Luca.

SELF-LOVE

ONE DAY, WHILE CLEANING THE mirror in his passage, I caught a glimpse of myself and was struck by how beautiful I was! It dawned on me that I wasn't in this relationship to learn from Luca; rather, he was there to show me that I was perfect exactly as I am. This was my road-to-Damascus moment, when I finally looked into the mirror and saw my beauty, my courage, my strengths, and accepted and embraced my flaws. I was moved to such intense love for myself that all I wanted to do was laugh and cry.

I didn't need anything more to make anyone love me. I was loved by Me! I realised that relationships are here to teach and push us to grow spiritually.

It was only when Luca finally gave in to my persistent begging for him to undertake a "mushroom journey" with me that I discovered the strong bond that bound us together. In the journey, he was a soldier and I was a Red Indian and we were fighting each other. I got the upper hand and he looked into my eyes, pleading with me not to kill him, as I brought my tomahawk down on his head and did kill him. In his journey, he asked God why we were together in this lifetime, and God told him to show the world that enemies can love each other. I then realised our meeting again and our marriage was a karmic debt that needed to be repaid.

Luca represented my dark side, that side that I suppressed, the one filled with insecurities and shame, the one I denied.

I began to appreciate and love Luca with all his faults and attributes, as I realised that he was just projecting his insecurities onto me. I realised that he was truly my opposite in every way and, through accepting and loving him unconditionally, I was accepting and loving myself unconditionally. I was whole. I no longer needed anyone to complete me!

I had travelled to more than fifty-two countries searching for love and belonging and found whatever I was searching for was always present.

When I said goodbye to Luca at the airport, I knew our journey was complete. My eyes filled with tears as I kissed him for the final time, silently thanking him for showing me how special I am and giving me the gift of self-love.

Insight:

We as humans are constantly searching for "the one" and relationships are there to show us who we are. It's a mirror for who we are and, as we outgrow that relationship/teacher, we will attract another teacher on every level of our spiritual growth. Ultimately, we will realise that we are "the one". There is no one out there who can make us whole; we were born whole! Luca had given me the gift of Self-Love!

SPIRITUAL JOURNEYS

MY SPIRITUAL CALLING BECAME MORE intense and I knew I could no longer avoid it, as no material or physical activities could fill that deep sense of knowing that I had a calling, a higher purpose! I began doing inner healing with visionary plants, particularly psilocybin mushrooms that open up your senses and deepen your connection to the spirit world. The weirdest things started happening; whenever I facilitated a journey with a client, I felt this birdlike creature inhabiting my body.

I knew it was a bird from the way my back arched and I couldn't sit up straight but had to crouch, and my stomach would blow up like a balloon. I saw in one of my journeys that I had the body of a human but a bird's head. I tried to make sense of this and guessed that it might be a phoenix or some bird-like creature. This creature spoke through me and passed on messages to my clients. It was only when, during a journey, one of my clients addressed me by the name "Horus" and told me I am completely gold, that the hundredweight penny dropped! Horus was the "bird" that inhabited my physical body. Before this incident, I did not know about Horus's existence.

More strange things began to happen. Whenever I was in a healing ceremony with a client, I found that I was channelling their higher power and received many messages on behalf of them. Some of these were from the I Am, Buddha, Goddess of Love, of Beauty, the Sun, Creation, and there were many more. Each of these deities would leave me with such profound clarity and love for myself and humanity.

Insight:
It seems like every human is entrusted with a higher purpose and they are guided by a higher power to achieve this purpose.

During most journeys I received messages that I was asked to share with everyone and on one of these journeys I was told to write a book and it should be called *Duality*, which conveys the "darkness and light" within. Darkness and Light coexist; one cannot exist without the other. Spiritual growth occurs in the darkness through suffering and pain, before we emerge into the light. We will then return to the darkness again. It's the dance of duality. There is no such thing as "good" or "bad", as both are essential to our growth. There are only consequences!

A few times during some of my journeys I was asked if I wanted to "come back", although I didn't know the place where I would be going back to. I experienced such intense love and beauty during these interactions. There was never any negative feedback, only that the answer to my suffering was that I should love myself. I was told many times that I came to earth to fulfil a purpose, but I had a choice to "come back" whenever I wanted.

I always answered emphatically that I didn't want to return and that I wanted to be Solly, Harry and Sammy's mother. The voice within would tell me to "Choose the reality that you've created"!

During my second journey, I was again a human with the face of a bird, sitting desolately on the ground with my head hung low on my chest. As I looked out onto my surroundings it was akin to the aftermath of a war, with dead bodies strewn across the field, mummies rising out of the ash walking around lifelessly. I asked my Father, "Why all the pain and suffering?" and He replied, "Until you stand up and rise, the suffering will continue".

I asked Him why my family and loved ones hurt and betrayed me and inflicted so much pain on me and His reply was, "What they did was only acting in their interest and you made it mean betrayal. They came to be your teachers in this lifetime and you have to thank them." Because our soul grows through suffering and pain, these "teachers" were lovingly pushing me further on the path towards self-love/enlightenment!

My Father said, "You are the chosen one; everything starts with you. I gave you dominion over the earth and all that's in it and that you can choose anything you desire, but you should rise and shine your light to the world, so others can shine their light."

Another profound journey took place at my house and my friends Ali and Ismail came to observe but did not partake of the mushrooms.

Five people participated, and I took a full dose of mushrooms along with them. The day was beautiful and sunny, so I left the group and went to lie on the grass, looking up to the sky. A short time later, I began to feel its effects. I started sobbing as the darkness and pain overwhelmed me. I begged my Father to forgive me, to stop my pain, and to allow me to be at peace. My Father responded in a kind voice. "I love you so much," but he insisted, "You must love yourself first". I was once again asked, "Do you want to come back?"

My eyes opened wide as I noticed the angels high up in the sky. I instinctively knew that they had come to fetch me. I jumped up and ran into the house, begging Ali to protect me as I did not want to go. However, I had already left my body and was looking down onto everyone as they all stared at this foreign object.

I could not get back into my body and repeated many times that I wanted to stay on earth.

Once again, this bird-like creature inhabited my body and for the first time, I asked him, "Who are you?"

He replied, "I am Horus. I am Jesus"

Ali and Ismail were dumbstruck and in awe of what they saw in the sky, and they gave me a full account of what they saw and experienced.

Ali's Experience of the Journey!

A FEW WEEKS LATER, LIZ told me about magic mushrooms. As a kid growing up in a relatively naïve society, I had never been exposed to drugs of any sort. Also, my recent meeting with Ayahuasca had confirmed that there was no need to pursue this pastime. "Mushrooms," she explained, "take you on a powerful journey but there is no throwing up. All your senses are heightened, and you are totally open to your subconscious thoughts. It's a mystical experience." This time I investigated the pros and cons. A lot depended on a happy and healthy mindset, the controlled dosage administered by someone who knew what they were doing and a safe, comfortable environment. Time and space seemed to be distorted and mentally partakers reported leaving this reality. There were also those who had experienced a bad trip, causing confusion, paranoia and anxiety.

Since I have never shown symptoms of depression, the positive spin off in dealing with suicidal behaviour were not foremost in my mind. I therefore distanced myself from her "journeys" until the day she requested that I bear witness to one that she was hosting - for inclusion in her book. This time I was totally alert and of sober mind, pen and pad poised.

I waited for two hours before arriving on the scene, to give the participants time to settle into their "journey". Horrified, I was confronted by Liz, who, instead of controlling the meeting, was wandering around in a stupor, staggering precariously close to an open fire.

I led her into the garden and watched her glazed, smiling face as she said over and over, "I am so beautiful, God loves me so much. I am his princess."

"Yeah, that's great," I responded, "but I'm sure he would appreciate you a lot more if you held on to this body a bit longer!" I left her to chat with Ismail, one of the husbands whose wife had taken mushrooms. He was pretty chilled about the whole thing and together we watched Liz take on a flattened-out yoga pose, picking at the grass and checking on the progress of ants.

Not long after, she started shouting for me. "Don't let them take me... don't let them take me." She became frantic. "Take me inside... they're coming to get me." Tears streamed down her cheeks as I pulled her into the house and tried to calm her down. She flattened her hands against the wall, with her back pressing the cold concrete.

"Who is coming Liz... where are they taking you?" I repeatedly asked, but ever so gently.

She continued to sob into my shoulder. "I don't want to go."

Ismail slowly approached. "You had better come and see this," he said quietly and led me back out into the garden. Pointing at the clouds just above us, he focused my attention on two round discs, hovering side by side. They were not moving in any direction, just hovering.

"Jeez," I spluttered, "is this for real, or are we imagining it?"

"You and I are the only ones who are not hallucinating so, yes, I think they are real," Ismail responded.

"Wow, no wonder Liz is so freaked out." We watched for at least ten minutes, half expecting the shapes to dissipate into drifting clouds, but they didn't. I made my way into the house and found Liz huddled in a foetal position, with fear distorting her huge, staring eyes.

"Liz," I spoke as calmly as I could, "you do not have to go anywhere; it's your choice. But you do have to make a decision."

She stood up. "I choose to remain here, on earth. I love my life, I love my family, I love my friends, I love you." Her voice strengthened as she reaffirmed each intention. I backed out of the room and joined Ismail. Within seconds, the two discs turned on edge and sped into the distance, leaving a hole. One day later, Liz had no recollection of the incident. I told her I would include it in her book but assured her that she was safe from the loony-bin because no one would believe the story.

THE EARTH

MY JOURNEY ON THE 22ND of June 2019. A few days before I had to depart to Italy for the summer, I decided to invite a few friends over to join me in a mushroom ceremony. I had no idea that it was the winter solstice as I do not follow the pagan calendar. We all sat around in a circle and said a silent prayer, then everyone found their space in the room and made themselves comfortable as we awaited the effects of the mushrooms.

As usual, I felt anxious in the beginning as I had no idea what I was going to experience on this journey. After about thirty minutes, the violent shivering started and I felt this energy/ entity entering my body.

"Who are you?" I asked and the voice answered, "I am the earth". It was sobbing, saying "The boys are killing me with their weapons and greed for power. Mothers, go back to nurturing your children; they need love. Stop trying to compete with the men. Be the mother you were born to be."

Then she went on to say, "You are my children; I speak and feel through you. I am your mother, but you are destroying me."

After she left, I was asked again, "Do you want to come back?"

I asked, "Back where?" I felt so much love from this female entity and, as she spoke, her words clarified everything for me when she replied, "You are Pleaidian. You have chosen to incarnate as a human because you love the earth so much."

She told me that the earth used to be part of their solar system and the earth is their sister planet. The earth did something that angered her father, who expelled her from the family, and now she will always be in pain. They wished for the earth to become part of their family again, but our beautiful planet is on its way to a black hole that will swallow the entire planet and its inhabitants.

Then, I found myself in the darkest black vortex, being pulled apart! If hell exists, then this must have been it! When I came out of the terrifying the black hole, I once again begged my Father for forgiveness and His loving answer was always the same: "I love you so much, but you have to love yourself".

The female voice started crying, repeating the words, "The Beast has won and only you can save the world".

"Who is the beast?" I asked.

"Money is the beast," she replied. "Money has taken over the world, and humans are worshipping money. Everything they do is with the intention of accumulating more and more money."

The greed for money has replaced the purpose every human came with to earth to fulfil. Each one of us was given a gift/ passion to share with the world, which is our purpose, but we have forgotten this in our quest to accumulate wealth. Our passion should be what we earn our money from.

"You have to save the earth from extinction and the only way to do this is by raising the vibration of humans and only love can do that," she said.

My voice was trembling as I whispered to her, "I am exhausted; I can't do this alone".

She responded, "Many came to walk this path along with you and they are all waiting for you to rise".

She went on to say, "The only way you can save your beloved planet is to raise your vibration as a collective human race and love is the only weapon in that endeavour - Self-love!"

No one will be left behind. I cannot rise without you, and you cannot rise without me. We are one!

THE ENTIRE UNIVERSE

AFTER A WHILE I DISCOVERED that I could transcend the earthly realm at will and was able to connect with the Pleaidians, who were especially present at night when I had trouble sleeping.

After receiving many teachings and recalling many things about their philosophy, I began to write about it. Whenever I contemplated something, I would get the answer immediately, as if I had a direct line to God.

One particular lesson gave me such clarity that it completely changed my perception of life. After telling me I was the entire universe, they then proceeded to show me in graphics and colours that each person is born perfect and that we don't need anything from the outside to make us whole. No one outside of ourselves can read our thoughts or feel our emotions; our only gift to the world is our word. Therefore, when we think a thought, it creates a reaction in our bodies, which causes an emotion, and this emotion directly affects our cells. Thus, if we have anger, hatred, bitterness, resentment or any other negative feelings towards someone or something, it negatively affects our cells, resulting in sickness and fear and stress.

The same is true when we feel joy, excitement, happiness and love for another person, animal or situation. These are our feelings that positively impact our cells and bodies, which in turn help us heal holistically.

We send out vibrations of energy from our thoughts and emotions into the universe, and this vibration attracts like energies. Therefore, when negative emotions are present or when we are in a spiritual state of low self-value, we will attract people and situations that will not value us. A person's external circumstances, surroundings, friends, partner and work are direct reflections of their self-worth. As much as we are an entire universe within, we are also connected to everyone and everything, which makes us One!

Our community, friends, family and environment all serve as mirrors for who we are and what we do. We learn from them by observing ourselves through their perspective. Thus, everyone and everything we come into contact with who has an impact on us provides us with insight into where we are in our journey to self-love.

As human, we are constantly trying to make sense of life, but life doesn't make sense, as all we are doing here is to learn through our physical experiences.

Through their philosophy, I came to see the beauty and love all around me and realised everyone and everything in the universe exists for my good, pushing me toward self-love. It made me realise how privileged I am to be a human, since we possess immense power. We possess the capacity to create any reality we desire. We can brighten the world, or we can darken it, as we see fit.

Each of us has been blessed with a unique gift that should be shared with the world.

HEALING JOURNEYS

PLANTS SUCH AS PSILOCYBIN MUSHROOMS and ayahuasca are spiritual gifts from God, and are here to heal mankind. These plants have the ability to strip away our stories and reveal our true essence, which is love!

Over the past five years, I have facilitated a few healing journeys with friends and people referred to me by other people.

I remember a few of them vividly as their healing was profound.

One of my clients was a successful businesswoman in her fifties who confided in me that, even though she was wealthy and successful, she frequently broke down in tears without reason. Everything was going well in her life, and she couldn't understand why she was so upset, but she couldn't control it.

While on her mushroom journey, she recalled aborting a baby when she was eighteen and never thinking about it again.

During the journey, the little baby came to her, and she asked for forgiveness and forgave herself, thereby relieving her of the guilt she had carried and completing her relationship with this soul. She was completely transformed after her journey, as she had released the shame and guilt that she had buried so deeply, but it had affected her in so many other areas of her life.

Similarly, another young man came to me struggling with grief after his mother in Zimbabwe had passed away, and he was unable to say goodbye to her. He was the youngest son, and he was consumed with guilt and sadness. During his journey, his mother came to him and hugged him, telling him how much she loved him. He had the opportunity to say goodbye and was complete with her passing. The transformation and light that shone on his face in the aftermath of this process is the reward I get from facilitating the healing process.

A few days before I was due to return to Italy, I decided to have my nails gelled and searched on Facebook for a home-based salon operator. There were many in my area but for some reason one particular advert jumped out at me. It was a bit further towards Muizenberg and without hesitation I made a booking. My GPS guided me to the back of the Muizenberg cemetery, where I found a woman with a bald head standing outside a small house waiting for me.

Upon entering her house, she ushered me to the back room where all her equipment was laid out on a table. During our conversation, she confided in me that she had a stage 4 brain cancer tumour and had three months to live. Her conversation was dominated by bitterness and anger towards her late mother and ex-husband.

The fact that I'd passed by about ten other salons on the way to her house made me wonder why I was sent there to have my nails done. I instinctively knew that God had sent me to her to help her with her illness. Having explained to her how I support and facilitate healing journeys, she was eager for me to assist her.

The following Saturday, she arrived promptly and began the inner journey. After a while, God instructed me to take her outside to receive the healing rays of the sun. In her journey, she was able to forgive her late mother and her ex-husband, and God told her that the tumour was all the negativity, bitterness and hatred that she had harboured for years before it eventually poisoned her body.

Throughout these experiences, it was made clear to me that sickness is internal, and no one can heal another as healing is also internal. We are the cause of our own illness with our negativity and darkness, and we alone are able to heal ourselves.

As humans, we don't want to be held accountable for our disease and place our health in the hands of doctors who can only treat the symptoms without dealing with the underlying cause, since illness is a message from the soul telling us to embrace and accept our darkness and transcend what keeps us trapped.

MADI

I HAD TO GO BACK to Como alone in 2021 and again no one could accompany me because of the Covid-19 restrictions. I looked forward to getting away from the pain and rejection suffered from my son Harry and his wife. His children had come to mean the world to me; they gave my life new meaning and I was mourning the loss of this relationship.

At three months old, Madi crept into my heart and all I wanted to do was love and protect this precious little baby. She was a happy child and would lie for hours playing and gurgling, I was bowled over by her. My relationship with this little girl grew strong and my life took on a new meaning with this child and through her I became a child again. We did fun things together and she was so eager to please. She especially wanted her mother's love and approval and would continuously try to do little things to make her mother happy.

Embracing Melanie as my own daughter, I became close friends with her. When she complained or was upset, I would put my son aside for her. I knew a happy Melanie meant a happy son and granddaughter, which made me happy.

When her little brother came along, Madi's life changed as she now had to share her parents with her baby brother. Melanie doted on her little boy, and I witnessed how Madi got blamed and punished when he got hurt and cried for no reason. With deep sadness, I watched as Melanie rejected Madi for little things, and how this once-confident and happy child became withdrawn and depressed. I tried to intervene and protect Madi as much as I could, but this led to Melanie refusing to talk to me, with the result that I no longer saw the children. Additionally, Madi was bullied at school and did not have any friends. At times, my heart wanted to break for her.

As parents, they were outraged that the school wasn't taking responsibility for the bullying, but they refused to accept that the bullying started at home.

Madi was treated by Melanie in a similar manner to how I was treated by my mother, who would put my brother first because he was a boy. He got privileges I only dreamt about. Madi stayed over in my flat on a Friday night, and as we were lying in bed one night, she told me she was planning to commit suicide. She made me promise not to tell her parents but said that she had told her school therapist.

When I asked her how she was going to do it, she described her plan to the last detail. I was shocked that a ten-year-old little girl, who should be laughing and having fun, wanted to end her life. I was caught between a rock and a hard place as I wanted to be there to help her but didn't want to cause her further problems.

A few weeks later, I happened to pass her school and spontaneously stopped, hoping to talk with her therapist. She wasn't immediately available but asked me to wait, as she also wanted to meet me since Madi had told her so much about me. Finally, she invited me into her office where I confided in her about Madi's threats. I told her about some incidences of rejection and emotional abuse I had witnessed and, feeling relieved, I left her office. I was surprised when a social worker called me a week later. She told me she had gotten my number from my son Solly and asked if she could ask me a few questions about my granddaughter, Madi. Although I wasn't sure what was going on, I decided to cooperate, especially if Madi would benefit from it.

A week later Harry told me the social worker had called him and Melanie to meet at their offices and asked if I could look after the children. I was happy to have them and we played our favourite game, hide and seek, which my little grandson loved.

A few hours later, their father came to fetch them, but he avoided looking at me. It never occurred to me that the therapist would have used my name in evidence against the parents. The report was filed under an alias, as she had gotten my details on FB. I was accused by Melanie of being a traitor and that she never wanted to see me again. I tried to convince her of my innocence, but she chose to believe that I had maliciously made the case against her. She banished me from their lives and told me that she no longer wanted me to have contact with her children. Despite my attempts to convince them of my innocence, Harry supported Melanie's decision.

Insight:
Whether it was the intention of the school therapist to deliberately use my name, I believe she only did what she thought best to save this little girl from the rejection and pain. She did it because she loved Madi. She was an angel who held Madi's hand through a painful time.

The parents seemed more indignant and offended at the inconvenience of going to the social worker's office to save their marriage than concerned for their child who was threatening to hurt herself!

I accepted that Melanie was not willing to look within herself and was not ready to deal with her childhood pain and trauma but would rather blame someone else. If crucifying me would benefit her and her children, then I know my pain was worth it.

These two children gave so much meaning to my life that I went into a deep and dark depression. I cried and mourned for almost a year, trying to make sense of this tragic incident.

It was only when I looked deeper at the lesson this incident brought that I realised that everything that happens to us is here to push us towards our purpose. And me trying to save Madi the pain also meant depriving her of the spiritual growth she had come to earth for.

One of the most painful lessons I have learned is that I am not here to save anyone, but only to love and support. By interfering in another soul's journey, you are doing them a huge injustice, since every soul came to earth for a purpose, which is to attain self-love and enlightenment.

The lesson here for me was love without attachment! Loving someone does not require that we need to be with them, but should support them with unconditional love.

SUMMER IN PARADISE

I LOOKED FORWARD TO SPENDING some time in my paradise, to reflect, heal and relax away from the emotional chaos in Cape Town.

In the beginning, it was a pleasure being on the *Beautiful Lake*, going for walks in the mountains and basking in the sun, but after a few weeks of having no personal contact with anyone I started slowly to spiral into a dark loneliness and depression. Solly told me, "Mom, do whatever you have to do to get you through this period".

Initially, I binged on sugar, but as usual guilt and shame soon followed, which convinced me it was time to heal my emotional eating crutch. It wasn't until I needed comfort and refused to give in to food that my anxiety soared, my heart rate increased, and I began to believe I was dying. Once I bit into the chocolate, I felt a familiar sense of reassurance and relief.

Then it suddenly dawned on me that I had to thank the food for comforting and loving me when I needed it most. After demonising food with guilt and shame, I learned to respect it and appreciate its comfort, love and support. As a result, I now savour and enjoy everything I eat, regardless of how healthy or unhealthy it is.

Insight:
As soon as I fully accepted and embraced my food and gambling addictions as part of who I was, instead of denying it, I was free of shame, guilt and self-punishment, and the addiction disappeared completely. No longer was I tempted to engage in this destructive behaviour as a means of avoidance. As a result, I started respecting and honouring my body as the sacred temple it is. Money took on a different meaning, since it was the by-product of the energy I spent on living my purpose.

My six months alone in my paradise were some of the loneliest of my life and I would not have made it without the comforting presence of God. When I wasn't able to share my paradise with others, it became my hell. While I am the entire universe, I am also connected to everything else! It taught me once again that there's duality in everything.

My heart ached to return to Cape Town, just to be able to connect with my people, my culture, my food and my home.

SAMMY BREAKS FREE

MY DAUGHTER, MY PRINCESS! I wanted nothing but the best for her. I tried to protect her as much as I could. Her father did not spend much time with her, and I tried hard to fill that gap. He didn't fetch her on weekends or take her out for play dates. On one of her birthdays, she and her friends waited all day for him to collect them, as he had promised to take them out on her birthday, but he never showed up.

As a proud mother, I attended her graduation from UCT, as did her father, but I had to beg him to attend. She looked beautiful and my heart swelled with pride. After the ceremony, she asked if we could go to one of our favourite restaurants for drinks. After an abusive outburst, her father refused to accompany us as he had to go home to avoid angering his wife. My heart broke seeing her pain and rejection and I just broke down and wept. I hated him for the way he had inflicted pain on my children.

He gave her money as a way of showing his love. Time and love were not on his agenda.

Throughout her life, Solly acted as a fatherly role model. It was his baby whom he took care of from the moment she was conceived. In fact, people thought he was her father when I was pregnant because he was so caring and protective of me.

Sammy is a beautiful, intelligent young woman who has a natural ability to write and speak. The world is her oyster and she could wave a wand and pick a star.

As a single mother, I often sacrificed my happiness to make Sammy's life as comfortable as possible. Sammy started going to discos when she turned fourteen and there were a number of nights when I stayed awake to wait for her return, only being able to sleep when I knew she was safely in bed. There were nights when she never came home, and I would run around the streets, visit police stations and even call hospitals to look for her, whilst her father was comfortably ensconced in his bed with his new family.

I tried in every way to make her life comfortable. Her wish was my command and I was her slave!

Although I tried hard to make up for her father's absence, she never appreciated what I did to make her life comfortable. In her life, my value was very low because I lacked money and status. Whenever her father spent an hour over lunch with her, her father's picture would be posted on FB or on her profile. Although I felt rejected, I only wanted to make my daughter happy, and I understood that she needed to spend time with her father in order to heal her abandonment issues.

After she graduated from UCT, Sammy decided to take a marketing course at Vega, which is one of the top marketing colleges in Cape Town. However, she had little ambition or direction. Sammy started acting very secretively, and I was only glad that she was living her life. On Sundays, she was never present, and her excuse was that she was recovering from a late night. Sammy became involved with a cocaine-addicted personal trainer, and I was worried that he might affect her negatively.

I tried to overlook this and thought that if she were happy then I could not judge her, so I accepted this man into my family. During Covid, Sammy came to live with me at my son-in-law's mountain house in Rhodes Drive, which he was renovating. However, I observed that Sammy became extremely excited when the builders arrived, and even rushed to greet them. I thought this was rather strange. I asked myself, "What did Sammy have in common with the builders and workers of Delft?"

While watching TV one night, one of the construction workers called her on her mobile. I was very surprised by this. However, I accepted her explanation that he was going to fix her door at her house in Constantia, as there couldn't possibly be any other reason for their interaction.

On a Sunday morning, Solly called me and told me that he had discovered that Sammy and this guy were having an affair.

She then called me hysterically, saying how ashamed she was and that he loved her. I was speechless! I was shocked to discover he was married, and that he had two illegitimate children with two different women for whom he refused to take responsibility.

The fact that she could have had anyone, yet wished to be with this man, was unfathomable to me. My first question was, "Why?"

She replied, "He loves me. Could you accept him?" I was extremely disappointed and felt terribly betrayed.

Insight:

Then it hit me like a physical blow! Was this how my grandmother felt when my mother had an affair with a "black" man? Is this why she despised me so much? After all, I was the physical manifestation of her daughter's infidelity and betrayal. Having hated and judged her harshly all my life, I suddenly felt compassion for her when I felt the same disappointment she must have felt.

There's always two sides to a story – Duality!

How could I have judged Sammy for her choice of man if that was exactly the kind of man I had married, her father. Her father's values and morals were of such a low standard and the only difference is that he had some money and this man didn't, but that didn't make him a better human being.

I saw so much potential in Sammy and I knew she was meant for big things in life. However, I now realise in hindsight that she did not see this in herself. She only wanted to be accepted and loved for who she was, not who I wanted her to be!

I acknowledge and have great respect for the fact that she had chosen to live her life regardless of the rejection and disapproval for the choice she made. With hindsight, I see the absolute desperation of her actions to banish me from her life as I was inhibiting her because of my expectations and judgments.

Insight:

What I wanted her to be is who I wanted to be! What I wanted for her is what I wanted for myself!

Her soul needed something completely different in order for her to grow.

How could I expect anything more than disrespect and disregard from Sammy, as that was how I was treating myself? In compromising myself and reducing my values I was portraying a mirror image of the way I was showing her how to treat me.

I was a martyr, not a mother!

In not valuing myself, I showed her that she shouldn't value herself either. In me not accepting who I was, I showed her that who she was is not acceptable!

When we compromise and sacrifice ourselves to make others happy, we devalue and dishonour who we are and in return we receive, disrespect, disregard, disloyalty.

Sammy was surely my teacher in teaching me about self-acceptance. It's because of her nudge that I've embraced who I am, and am living my purpose regardless of what others think or say. When I accept who I am, I give others permission to accept who they authentically are.

As I arrived back home from Italy and having closed the door on my marriage, I apologised and begged Harry for forgiveness for something I did not do to either him or his wife. They refused to let me back into their lives, so I had no choice but to painfully close the doors on those relationships.

With much sadness and resignation, I realised that my children were never mine. They came through me, and we've walked our journeys together, and now I had to let them go to walk their own path. My expectations of how a mother should be treated is what caused me pain. They had chosen to live their lives in the way that suits them, and I have accepted that they too are on the same journey to self-love and their soul will attract situations and people who will push them to grow.

COMING HOME

AFTER SETTING FOOT BACK ON South African soil, I felt as if I could have kissed the ground. It welcomed me with open arms. In the past, I looked forward to seeing my family and felt waves of nostalgia when there was no familiar face to welcome me. However, the joys of being amongst people with the same language made me feel at home. Suddenly, the squatter camps which once appalled me were a sight of familiarity, the beggars and sellers who before were an irritation were my people.

I acknowledged the courage of street people, drug addicts, alcoholics and those with other destructive behaviours who ventured into the darkness to grow spiritually. I respected and supported their journeys with compassion and love.

I embraced this country with its racialism, poverty and suffering. It is where I was born and where ultimately I belong. I am extremely proud to be a woman from South Africa and began accepting my coloured heritage: the language, the jokes that only a coloured person can appreciate, the generosity of my people so ready to please at their expense. I got to see how we accepted the label of unworthiness and mediocrity and realised that this was our journey in this lifetime. As a community, our lesson is to learn self-worth and we will all get to that stage eventually where we realise that we are perfect and only self-acceptance can do that!

My old labels of "not good enough, mediocre and unworthy" were no longer applicable. I could choose my own labels!

My now motto has become, "Laugh, Love, Live!"

Since I was no longer compelled to run from my darkness and shame, and the family I once believed belonged to me no longer exists, I now embrace humanity as my family, and the earth as my home. I belong! I have finally returned to my home, to Me!

I have seen life from both sides: I have been the maid and the madam, the master and beggar, the abused and the abuser, the child and mother, the student and teacher.

My journey of life has prepared me for the purpose for which I was born, and I have no choice but to embrace it. When I closed the doors on my loved ones, and my familiar past life, the next door already stood waiting for me.

I wish to show humanity that they are only love in its dark and light forms, since love is the only reality.

Duality is who we are!

My life story of suffering and pain was necessary for my growth, so I could shine my light so others could shine theirs as well.

To live our truth is to live the Highest Truth!

TEACHERS

WE ARE ALL SOULS ON a journey to self-Love, and the gift of spiritual growth lies in the pain and suffering. All the people and situations in my life served as loving teachers, pushing me toward loving myself.

No one in my life entered my life by accident. They came with a gift. Every incident of betrayal, dishonesty, pain and suffering that I experienced, were lessons that my soul needed to grow. No one is to blame, as everyone who caused me pain came as a teacher. I am grateful to each and every one who walked this journey with me, including my angels, who held my hand throughout without judgement. One of my greatest teachers, Harry, gave me the gift of unconditional love, to love without attachment or expectations.

The Pleiadeans, my spiritual teachers, taught me that I'm the entire universe and self-love is the answer.

The love I was searching for was always there, just waiting to be discovered. It was ME I was searching for!

No more apologising for who I am, no more compromising to belong, no more beating myself up for my actions. Only self-acceptance and self-love awaits me. I ran from me for so long and now I've embraced who I am, my darkness, my addictions, mediocrity, shame, anxiety, inadequacies, sadness and all the other insecurities as well as my light, my beauty, playfulness, laughter, joy...

I am darkness and light; I am love! I am whole! I am duality!

THE NEW WORLD

Duality Messages from Pleiadians to Liz on "The New World" as shared with Ali.

"I received clarity on the way forward. I saw you are a part of the new world. There is an urgency for us to understand it and share the messages with humanity. I was told that I am a messenger to bring the Truth to the people and that I would be supported by so many others along the way. The release of the book has been a trigger for me to step over and glimpse the New World.

I haven't slept for two days. The magnitude and enormity of this journey and the role I am expected to fulfil have been revealed and have hit me hard. I am experiencing fear, insecurities, and anxiety on another level.

I was told that we have made this world, and we are all responsible. We tell ourselves that it is 'the Russians, the Americans, the government,' always them, never us. But we have collectively created this reality.

THE WAR WITHIN HAS BECOME THE WAR WITHOUT.

The world has been sustained by war. After war comes peace and then another war and peace and so on. We have perpetuated this cycle for eons, and in this cycle, we have destroyed Mother Earth and, in doing so, we have destroyed ourselves.

Dark... Light... Dark... Light... DUALITY

They said, "There is no more time. This war and peace cycle must stop right now if we want to save our planet! There will always be duality but it will no longer result in a war. Instead, it will be about acceptance and tolerance of each other, knowing that we are One! We are the darkness and the light and we must embrace our duality instead of fighting our darkness".

And so, the NEW WORLD has opened, and I need to share with you what it looks like. How it will occur to us as human beings. You and I together share the responsibility to take humanity into this New World": a world where our actions are motivated by compassion and love. Where Respect and Honour for ourselves and others are inherent traits and acceptance and non-judgement form the foundation of our belief

THE END

THANKS!

I AM EXTREMELY GRATEFUL TO my dear friend Ali, who was the catalyst for me finally completing this book. Thank you for your unconditional support and love throughout this entire process.

THANKS TOO TO:

NEIL, MY FRIEND WHO ASSISTED and supported me throughout this journey without judgement.

Saleh, my son, who inspired and encouraged me to speak my truth.

And God, Who loved and carried me when I was too weak to stand.

www.ingramcontent.com/pod-product-compliance
Lightning Source LLC
Chambersburg PA
CBHW030925090426
42737CB00007B/322